Cruising
the
San Juan
Islands

Also by Bruce Calhoun

Northwest Passages, Volume I

Northwest Passages, Volume II

Mac and the Princess

Cruising the San Juan Islands

By Bruce Calhoun

Revised and updated by Dave Calhoun

WEATHERLY PRESS
BELLEVUE, WASHINGTON

ISBN 0-935727-07-8

The first edition of this book was published in 1973 by Sea Publications, Inc.

Cover photo of Reid Harbor by John Lund

Editorial assistance by Carolyn Threadgill

Design and production by Joan Kohl and Byron Canfield

Printed in the United States of America
 2 3 4 5 6 7 8 9 0

Published by Weatherly Press Division
Robert Hale & Co. Inc.
1803 132nd Ave. NE, Suite 4
Bellevue, WA 98005
USA

Dedication

This book is dedicated to my parents, whose many sacrifices during my childhood and youth made it possible for me to nurture a love of the sea, learn to know and enjoy boating, and develop a keen appreciation of nature in all her many moods.

B.C.

This second edition is dedicated to *my* parents, who, during my growing-up years, loaded all us kids into the family boat and spent the entire summer cruising in the Pacific Northwest. I remember only the good times, the quiet anchorages, and the spirit of exploration those summers afloat gave me.

D.C.

Turn Island

Contents

Foreword

An introduction from the author is hardly necessary, for the book itself says it all. It is my hope and intention that these pages may help others to enjoy the special magic of the San Juans by sharing with them whatever knowledge I have accumulated in three decades of cruising among the islands. With so much to enjoy in this lovely archipelago, there is no doubt much has been left out. But if these words can help other yachtsmen to a fuller appreciation of the many attributes of the San Juans, the effort will have achieved its purpose and this portion of the Pacific Northwest's finest cruising waters in the world will continue to grow in popularity.

—*Bruce Calhoun*

Publisher's Introduction

Cruising the San Juan Islands was first published in 1973, and until it went out of print in the early 1980's it was the only cruising guide available for the San Juan Islands. During those 10 years or so, thousands of families learned local history and safely navigated the islands with this book open in the cockpit.

A couple years ago, Bruce Calhoun's son Dave approached me at the Seattle Boat Show, and suggested that he update his father's book. The previous publisher had no plans to reprint, and graciously returned the rights. We began work with Dave to update the book. Dave, who lives with his wife and family on Orcas Island, revisited by boat and car the places mentioned in the book, and either verified that nothing had changed or made the needed changes. He also took a large number of photos to replace photos no longer appropriate.

The book has been updated with the very latest NOAA charts. Even though the charts are for reference only and not for navigation, we felt it best to use the latest versions available.

Aerial photos are both entertaining and useful in a cruising guide, and we decided to make the considerable investment in aerials just for this edition. Chris Eden of Eden Arts took the pictures, and Dick Britton flew the plane.

A number of additions and production changes were made to help the reader with this new edition. At the beginning of each chapter a "locator map" shows the area covered in that chapter. Beneath the locator map the principal bays, points, passages, dangers, and towns are listed, so the reader can quickly see what the chapter covers.

In addition, **bold type** is used to highlight place names. A person skimming to find certain information should be able to find it more easily. Bold type was inserted only where it seemed relevant. If, for instance, a particular bay was mentioned just in passing, we did not call attention to it.

Bold italic type is used to highlight piloting information, usually of a cautionary nature. Bruce Calhoun was an adventuresome cruiser. Tricky passages were challenges to his skills, and he liked to poke his nose into places the more timid would avoid. His approach comes through clearly in the book. Most often, Bruce's cautions tell the skipper how to avoid trouble while seeing everything that can be seen. It is a "can-do" attitude that gets the most out of cruising.

Many of the photos in this updated edition were included in the first edition, and in some of them the reader will see a vertical black line. This is because the original art has been lost, and we reused negatives created for the printing process. In the first edition, some of the photos extended across two pages, but the design of this revised edition did not allow the same treatment. The two halves of the earlier negatives were butted together as carefully as possible, but the vertical lines inevitably resulted.

Bruce Calhoun was born in Minneapolis in 1908. As a young man he worked his way west, finding jobs as an announcer in radio stations along the way. Bruce had a life-long interest in boats, and in 1960 he was offered the job as Northwest manager for *Sea* magazine, a position he held for 13 years.

Bruce was universally liked and respected during those years with *Sea.* He managed the delicate task of both selling the ads and writing the articles for the Northwest section. Too often in this situation, the ad salesman will write articles that are little more than glowing reports about ad clients. From the magazine's point of view, however, the opposite situation is worse: most writers can't sell ads. But Bruce could do both. He loved boats and boating so completely that he could write about them with honesty and enthusiasm, and he was a good enough businessman that he could sell the ads that paid for the Northwest office. He liked to say that he was being paid to pursue his hobby.

Bruce even helped his competitors. When other yachting publications needed news reports or photos of an event Bruce was covering, the reports and photos were provided without question. With that kind of attitude, he got the same courtesies in return. Local yachting press professionals recall Bruce Calhoun's days at *Sea* with warmth and fondness.

Bruce Calhoun retired from *Sea* in 1973. A large corporation had bought the magazine, and it no longer needed a Northwest office run by a dedicated boatman who swapped pictures with competitors. In 1975 Bruce moved to Eastsound, on Orcas Island, and cruised his boat, *Alldun,* throughout the islands. He continued to write, placing a number of articles in *Sea* and other magazines. And he finished another book, *Mac and the Princess,* the story of Mac MacDonald and MacDonald's beloved Princess Louisa Inlet. Bruce had hopes of writing other books, but they were not to be. He died of leukemia in 1980.

I hope you will find this new edition of Bruce Calhoun's *Cruising the San Juan Islands* both interesting and useful. Bruce's love of cruising and his passion for these islands are apparent on every page. Bruce is gone now, but the spirit of discovery and adventure that he found so exciting still exists. So go slow, be curious, watch the weather, and have a memorable cruise.

—*Bob Hale*
Weatherly Press

C H A P T E R

1

THE MAGIC OF THE SAN JUANS

Walt Woodward's *Big Toot II* at anchor in a
small bay on the southeast end of Matia Island,
a wildlife refuge in the San Juan Islands.
A state marine park mooring float is on
Matia Island's northwest side.

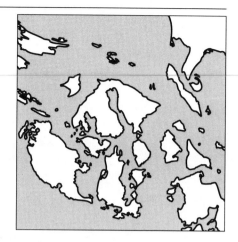

Geography
Geology
History
Charm

he visitor should not try to count them. Even the experts cannot agree on the number of islands contained in that delightful archipelago in Washington Sound known as the San Juan Islands.

It depends, of course, on what is counted and how and when it is counted. At low tide various totals—all well over 750—are given for the islands (twin or double islands bearing one name), rocks, and reefs. As the rising tide covers some of them, the number of islands shrinks to something over 450. There is even disagreement on the number of those important enough to have names, but 172 seems to be the figure most commonly accepted for this category.

The number, however, is not really important. What is important is the beauty and charm of the entire area. The skipper, his family, and guests are imbued with a spirit of peace and repose which diminishes the cares, the pressures, and the tensions of work-a-day city life.

To this serenity of the soul is added an easily perceptible sharpening of the senses. Colors seem to become more vivid as the eyes record the grandeur of this wonderland with its gallery of magnificent pictures unfolding around every bend in the waterway. Untainted salt air and pine-scented breezes invite deep breathing. Ears quickly become attuned to the cry of a seagull, the twittering of birds, and the gentle lap of wavelets against the hull of an anchored boat. Appetites quicken at the taste of barbecued salmon or of shellfish brought back from an afternoon of dinghy adventuring. Even the sense of touch is heightened by bare feet on a warm sandy beach, a dip in the invigorating salt water, or the smooth texture of agates or driftwood picked up on the wave-washed shores.

Finally, there is the sheer joy of cruising, of being aboard a good boat, of meeting old friends and finding new ones, of bedding down for the night to be gently rocked to sleep in a cozy little cove, of enjoying the hospitality of the island people who experience this life the year-round and are willing to share it with visitors.

These are just a few of the ingredients making up that heady potion called the Magic of the Islands, which "takes over" the moment one enters the waters of the San Juans.

The Indians found the islands first. Members of the Lummi tribe lived on San Juan and Orcas islands long before the days of recorded

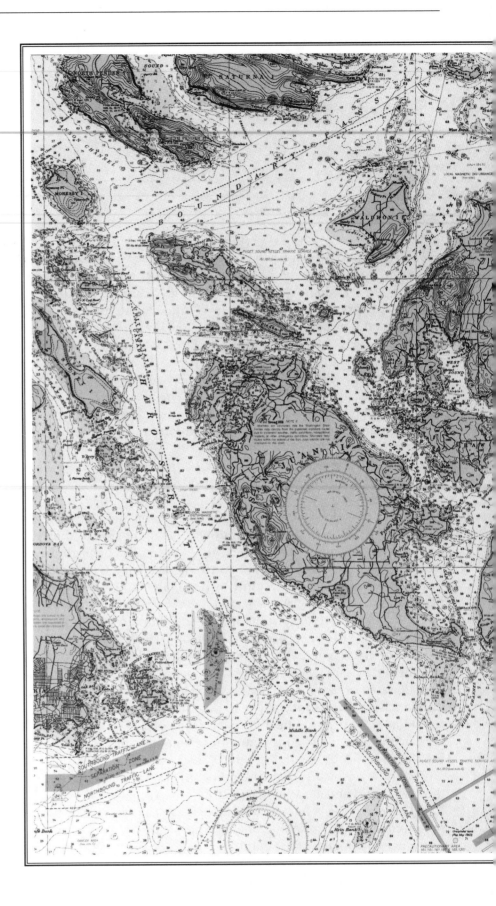

NOAA chart 18421, the most-commonly carried chart of the San Juan Islands. The chart provides an excellent overview. The prudent skipper, however, also will invest in the larger-scale charts 18427, 18433, and 18434. These charts show smaller areas of the islands in much greater detail ("Large scale, large detail"). They make tricky passages easier, and reveal interesting anchorages that are easily overlooked on the smaller-scale chart 18421.

Not intended for navigation

history. Probably the first Europeans to lay eyes on the San Juans, if only from a distance, were the Spaniards Manuel Quimper, Gonzalo Lopez de Haro, and Juan Carrusco. Carrusco probably made the nearest approach to the islands when he explored the entrance of Haro Strait and a part of Rosario Strait in 1790.

The following year Francisco Eliza sent Juan Pantoja y Arriaga aboard the *Santa Saturnina* for a more detailed exploration of the islands. Arriaga reached what are now the Canadian Gulf Islands, but saw only the northern fringe islands of the San Juans.

It was Lieutenant William Broughton, a member of Captain Vancouver's expedition in 1792, who got the first close look at the interior islands. Commanding the *Chatham*, Broughton sailed through Cattle Pass into Griffin Bay, around Turn Island, up Upright Channel and into East Sound. Meanwhile, a party in two small boats went up San Juan Channel. Harney Channel, Blind Bay, and Lopez Sound were explored before they traveled, either through Obstruction Pass or Peavine Pass, into Rosario Strait for a look at Lummi, Sinclair, and Cypress islands.

The *Chatham* then rejoined Vancouver's *Discovery* off Bainbridge Island's Restoration Point. Some days later the expedition returned to the San Juans, heading for Strawberry Bay on Cypress Island. The *Discovery* arrived and anchored, but the *Chatham*, meeting strong crosscurrents, was set onto the rocky south shore of the island. The line of the hastily thrown stream anchor broke. Although the crew spent considerable time dragging for the lost anchor, they did not recover it. No doubt that anchor is still there, waiting for some adventuresome diver to make what would certainly be the historical find of the century.

Broughton also lost a sounding lead off the southeast shore of Orcas Island while trying to work the *Chatham* off the rocks there. Here is another possible historical objective for divers, but a difficult one due to the rocky shore and strong current.

Today, as we cruise among these lovely "rocky isles, well cloath'd with wood," as Broughton described them, and revel in their mood of tranquil relaxation, we find it difficult to realize that peace and quiet have not always prevailed here. Names like Massacre Bay, Skull Island and Victim Island recall bloody Indian encounters when marauding Haidas swept down from the north to raid the Lummis in West Sound.

There was also the famous Pig War on San Juan Island during the boundary dispute of the 1800's. This was a bloodless engagement with the pig the only shooting casualty, but it generated much that cannot be classified as peace and quiet. The Pig War days were followed by a period that saw island life dominated by a rough frontier element centering around boisterous old San Juan Town and, later, a saloon-filled Friday Harbor.

With innumerable hidden coves and bays connected by an intricate system of channels and passages, the San Juan Islands were a natural headquarters for smugglers who dealt in opium, diamonds, silk, wool, and the illegal import of Chinese labor. During the "noble experiment" of the 1920's and early 1930's, bootleggers found the

area ideally suited to their operations, and again there was plenty of action in the islands, with shots fired and even murder.

Anyone wanting full details on this exciting period in Northwest history will find the story well researched and documented in David Richardson's excellent book *Pig War Islands*.

Occasionally while boating in this area one gets the feeling of cruising among mountain peaks. Actually that is what one is doing. Geologists tell us that the islands—not only the San Juans but all of the northwestern coastal islands, from Puget Sound to southeast Alaska—are part of a drowned mountain range. According to geologists, this part of the continental coast was once bounded by a series of rugged mountains. A valley lay between these mountains and another, even higher, range of mountains inland, with deep canyons and passes cut by ancient rivers.

Sometime in the distant past, the outer mountains tilted seaward and sank. The tops thus became the islands we know today. The sea poured inland, filling the valleys and invading the inner mountains, to form the long inlets from the canyons and ravines of old riverbeds.

In the San Juan group, the highest summit is Mt. Constitution, rising to 2,409 feet. The lowest charted depth is 195 fathoms, although a depth of 226 fathoms, or 1,356 feet, has been reported near Stuart Island in Haro Strait. Thus it is a total of 3,765 feet from the deepest submerged valley to the top of Mt. Constitution.

Friday Harbor, on San Juan Island, is the commercial center of the islands. A customs dock, ample guest moorage, fuel, showers, and shopping make the town a popular stopover.

The beautiful San Juan "constellation" in this galaxy of islands is grouped around the four larger islands—Orcas, San Juan, Lopez, and Shaw—with the smaller islands intermingled or sparkling on the fringes. It seems a shame that the chart makers have discarded the name of Washington Sound for the waters from Vancouver Island to the mainland, between the Strait of Georgia and the Strait of Juan de Fuca. This means that for most yachtsmen, Puget Sound has been stretched to include everything from Olympia to the international boundary.

Striking contrasts are found in the San Juans. There are protected sandy beaches as well as abrupt rocky cliffs that rise directly from the waterline. There are lush timbered hills and mountains, and pastoral meadows full of wildflowers. Quaint old settlements stand

Two boats negotiate Pole Pass, the narrowest pass in the islands. Pole Pass lies between Crane Island and Orcas Island.

guard at the heads of quiet harbors, while, to the newcomer, peaceful little coves appear as if they had just been discovered.

The San Juan Islands offer a water-oriented experience that many Northwesterners take for granted, while out-of-state visitors wax rhapsodic over the many miles of varied coastline indented by scores of scenic bays and coves. The ever-changing panorama of emerald isles, wooded hills, narrow passageways, and open beaches is set in clear, beautiful waters against a grandiose backdrop of distant snow-covered mountain peaks. Visitors who go ashore can find oysters, clams, and intriguing rocks and bits of driftwood.

There is no monotony in cruising in the San Juan Islands, even for skippers who return year after year to cross and recross the same waterways and visit the same favorite spots. Each day is as fresh and new as the sand just uncovered by the ebbing tide. One forgets the clock and wishes he had time to forget the calendar. It is not so much what is seen as what is felt when the magic of the islands has engulfed the senses.

Cruising pleasure has been greatly enhanced during the past two decades by an increasing number of state marine parks. In the early 1950's, Washington State Parks and Recreation Commission officials realized that boating was fast becoming a major part of the recreation picture. Recognizing that the San Juans offered an oustanding opportunity to enjoy this activity, they moved at once to develop the unique kind of park, a marine park, which can be reached only by boat.

The commission, with some assistance from the local yachting fraternity, has established 17 of these parks in the San Juans area. Also recognizing that a major goal must be the acquisition of suitable property for parks before such property becomes unavailable or too expensive, the commission has purchased more than 20 park sites in the islands and is acquiring others as fast as possible. While many of these sites may wait some time for development and others may never be developed, their existence promises the cruising family a bright future as well as an immediate opportunity to go ashore without encroaching on private property.

Most of the state marine parks provide sheltered harbors, with moorage buoys, docks, and floats. Most have picnic sites and campsites, camp-type cooking stoves and barbecue pits, toilet facilities, and trails for hiking. Some of the parks provide drinking water, but to be sure of having it, cruising families should bring their own supply. Swimming can be enjoyed at some of these sites and oysters, clams, and crabs are frequently found.

The Washington State Parks and Recreation Commission receives many requests from the boating public to avoid too much development. Many boatmen prefer to camp out in wilderness surroundings that have been left as much as possible the way nature created them. Officials take these requests into consideration in their development planning for these areas.

For those who want more comforts than raw nature can provide, the islands offer a number of marinas well equipped with facilities and several well-known yachting-oriented resorts which will be discussed later in this book.

In this book I often use the term "beachbcombing," so perhaps I should clarify my meaning of the term. While beachcombing usually suggests walking along a beach in search of driftwood or other treasures thrown up by the sea, it has come to be used by yachtsmen as slang for running a boat as close as possible to the shore. I use it here in the latter sense and do not mean to suggest trespassing on a private beach.

Cruising in Northwest waters has become a way of life for thousands, even those who can spend only a short vacation and selected long weekends here. Cruising in the San Juans is a special

West Sound's exit, with Double Island on the left side of the photo. Protected anchorage can be found in the small bay where the dock is located.

way of life. It may be negotiating winding channels between forested or rock-rimmed isles as one's wake scouts the shoreline. It may be discovering a new waterway, or exploring more intimately a beach or bay. It may be just relaxing in the sun, watching the graceful undulations of a school of jellyfish, while overhead a seagull complains about his hunger pains.

By late afternoon or early evening it is time for the boating family to find a suitable harbor. The late Captain Chris Wilkins, who sailed his charter boat in the San Juans for many years and lived on Christmas Island in Fossil Bay, wrote some lovely thoughts about harbors, which I quote in part, with his permission:

> It is the land which makes the yachtsman appreciate the sea just as most emphatically the opposite can be true. Those of us who cruise love the water but we also love harbors. Water is a highway, a road that is sometimes smooth, sometimes rough. It leads

everywhere from your home port to the most remote islands....
Always there is an end to a passage.

Nothing about cruising can be nicer than a snug harbor.
Each harbor is different, each becomes a part of your cruising
memories. One you approach carefully, feeling a way across
unmarked waters with lead plummeting from the bow as you
grope close under the protection of the lee of the shore. You
watch carefully for a hidden rock and maneuver clear of the other
boats trying to locate a bit of ocean bottom that will be hospitable
to your anchor.

Another harbor you approach with confidence. With fine
sweep and dash you come right in, certain of depth and swinging
room. You have been here before....

Each harbor is an achievement—a goal that you have at-
tained. It is the reward of serious thought, effort and skill. You left
the shore, you made the passage, you have come back to shore.
Dropping the anchor brings a sense of completion whether the
voyage was between continents or the banks of a lake....

The dark of the summer night comes late in the San Juans. As
we sit languidly in the cockpit, letting a grilled steak or seafood dinner
digest, we watch the yellow-orange sun being washed beyond the
shore of the horizon by the soft pastel waves of its own reflected light.
Later, the night sky sparkles with the confetti of constellations preparing to herald the arrival of her majesty, the moon. Somewhere,
through the trees on the point, a long white finger of light slices into
the darkness every 15 seconds, a beacon to guide those who have not
yet arrived at their harbor.

Recounting the pleasures of another day, we mentally tick off the
days left in our cruise schedule. No matter how long that schedule
may be, it is much too short. Reluctantly we head for the bunk, loathe
to leave the beauty of a night in the San Juans but aware that another
day approaches in which we can enjoy all of the charms and magic of
this lovely fleet of islands securely anchored in a protected inland sea.

2

GATEWAYS TO THE SAN JUANS

The Deception Pass bridge, with Deception Pass below. The pass is deceptively quiet. From the high-water mark on the rocks, the photo appears to have been taken at low slack water.

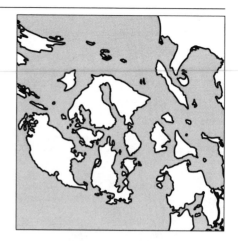

*Admiralty Inlet
Saratoga Passage
Skagit Bay
Deception Pass
Swinomish Channel
Haro Strait
Plumper Sound*

Practically every boatman in the Pacific Northwest knows where the San Juan Islands are located. However, thousands of skippers—newcomers and visitors from southern and eastern ports—plan to cruise this area. This chapter is written primarily for them.

The archipelago of these lovely, charmed isles is located in Washington Sound. Many people may not be able to find this sound because charts have dropped the name. The sound lies between the southern end of Vancouver Island on the west and the mainland on the east, with the Strait of Georgia on the north and the Strait of Juan de Fuca on the south.

There are many gateways into this cruising paradise and the choice of entryway is dependent on several factors. Since Seattle is often called the "Boating Capital of the World," and many of those cruising the San Juans come from the Puget Sound area, let's look first at possible routes from the south.

Boats from Olympia, Tacoma, and way points will head down sound, perhaps stopping at Seattle for the night. The phrase "down sound" is used deliberately for two reasons. A sound, like a bay, can have a "head" and the approaches to the head are known as the "upper" part of the sound, regardless of their compass direction.

In the days of sailing ships, skippers most often found themselves beating into the wind as they headed south to the upper sound. Going the other way they coasted easily, seemingly downhill, so they spoke of sailing "up sound" on the southerly trip and "down sound" when sailing north.

It is interesting to note that Puget Sound, as charted by Captain George Vancouver, and named by Vancouver in honor of his lieutenant, Peter Puget, designated those waters below Tacoma's Point Defiance. Common usage and the chart makers have extended the boundaries, first to Seattle, then up to Foulweather Bluff and, today, Puget Sound is generally considered to include Admiralty Inlet. Therefore, the sound now runs from the Strait of Juan de Fuca (at Point Wilson) to Olympia. Some people include the San Juan Islands but this is incorrect.

There are many good stopover points other than Seattle for those coming from the south-sound ports. Some skippers like to go into

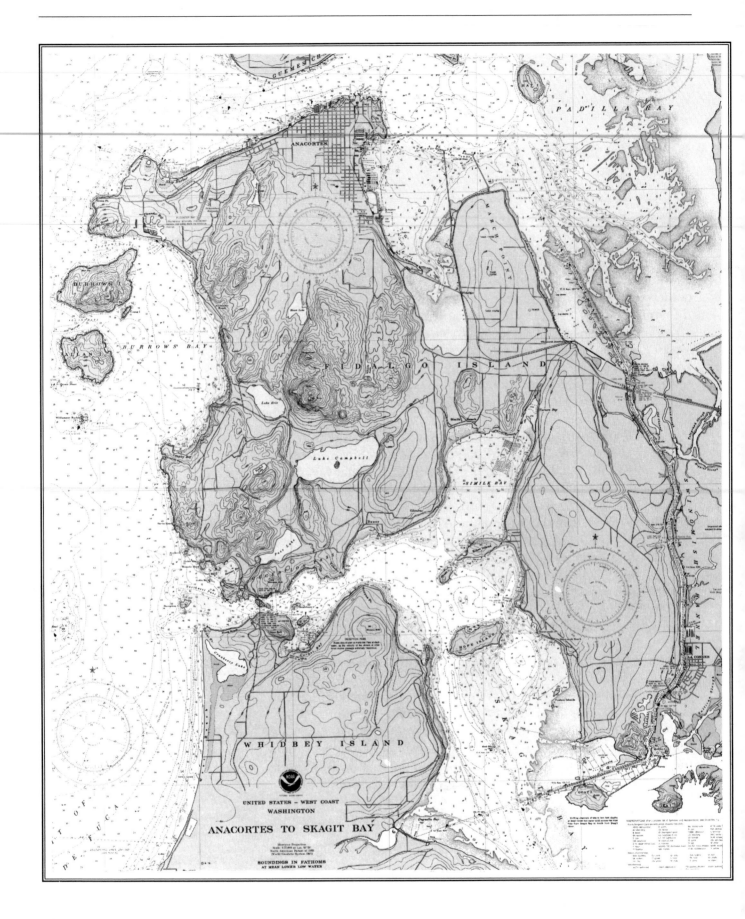

UNITED STATES — WEST COAST
WASHINGTON

ANACORTES TO SKAGIT BAY

Mercator Projection
Scale 1:25,000 at Lat. 48°30′
North American Datum of 1983
(World Geodetic System 1984)

SOUNDINGS IN FATHOMS
AT MEAN LOWER LOW WATER

bays in the Bremerton area, while others choose Poulsbo, Manzanita Bay, Miller Bay, Port Madison, Kingston, or Edmonds.

From Seattle's Shilshole Bay, it is approximately 13 miles to Possession Point, the southern tip of Whidbey Island. Here the skipper has a choice of two routes. Sailors and those with good sea boats often decide to go through **Admiralty Inlet** and cross the **Strait of Juan de Fuca** to **Haro Strait**, **Cattle Pass**, or **Rosario Strait**. Cattle Pass will not be found on the charts. It is charted as **Middle Channel**, but this narrow passage into San Juan Channel at Cattle Point, between San Juan and Lopez islands—again through popular usage—has become better known as Cattle Pass.

This is not a route to be chosen lightly. Violent tide rips often occur off Point Wilson. The same is true of the waters outside Cattle Pass. The waters of the Strait of Juan de Fuca can be mirror smooth or they can give the skipper a beating he will not care to take a second time. Prevailing winds in the summer are from the ocean to the west, and some sailors say the winds make up about 9:00 a.m., noon, or 3:00 p.m. When they blow, they can build up a sea that is mighty uncomfortable. So, in picking this route, *the boatman should consider carefully the weather, the seaworthiness of his boat, its speed, and his own abilities as a seaman.* It is approximately 22 miles across the strait from Point Wilson to the protected waters on the other side.

Popular stopovers on this route are **Port Ludlow**, **Mats Mats Bay**, **Mystery Bay** in Kilisut Harbor, and **Port Townsend**, which has two small boat harbors. Some skippers will choose **Keystone Harbor**, on Whidbey Island, but they must be ready for the early-morning departure of the ferry that runs to Port Townsend.

Probably the majority of skippers heading for the islands will choose the more protected inland route through **Possession Sound**, **Saratoga Passage**, and Skagit Bay. Although winds can whip through there, it is usually a comfortable trip. Those with slower boats, or from mid- or south-sound departure points, can find good layovers at **Everett**, **Gedney (Hat) Island**, **Tulalip Bay**, **Langley**, **Coupeville**, or **Utsalady**.

In Skagit Bay one has a choice of two routes. The more popular route is into **Rosario Strait** via **Deception Pass**. The alternative route swings to the east at **Goat Island**, then north through the **Swinomish Channel**, and into **Padilla Bay**.

A word of caution should be noted for the run through Skagit Bay. A good portion of Skagit Bay is shallow, with depths of only a foot or two in some places. The channel, however, has plenty of water and the trick is to stay in the channel. It is well marked, and for the first trip or two, *the skipper would be wise to favor the middle and pay close attention to large-scale chart 18427.*

When entering Skagit Bay one naturally looks for red nun buoy N "2." Many skippers, including myself, seem to have trouble locating that buoy. When we do, it does not appear to be where the chart says it will be found. The easiest way is to head almost on the **Strawberry Point Light** and keep fairly well in on that shoreline. Skippers are advised not to beachcomb, for there are rocks along the shore, but there is sufficient water just a short bit off. *You will be safe following this*

A look at the north end of Skagit Bay, showing both the Swinomish Channel and Deception Pass. The Skagit River has created extensive shoaling in the eastern part, and at low tide vessels must keep well west of the buoys to assure sufficient depth. Also note shoaling in Padilla Bay, in the upper right corner. The dredged channel must be followed, and vessels are well-advised to keep clear of the channel's edges.

Not intended for navigation

An overview looking from east to west,
with the town of LaConner lower center.

1 Whidbey Island
2 Allan Island
3 Burrows Island
4 Fidalgo Island
5 Cypress Island
6 Anacortes
7 Guemes Island
8 Sinclair Island.

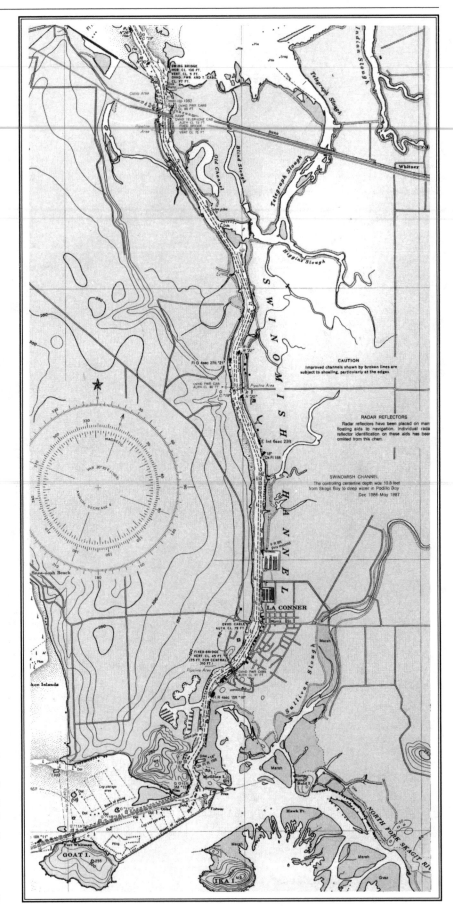

The Swinomish Channel is often used by skippers cruising between Seattle and Bellingham. It is generally calm and has a depth of 9 feet. The pioneer town of LaConner is near the southern end. Public moorage is available at the north end of LaConner, and it is but a short walk from the moorage to the town's shops and restaurants. Watch your wake when passing LaConner.

Not intended for navigation

16

The southern entrance to the Swinomish Channel is a dredged channel through mudflats. The wise skipper will not stray from the marked channel.

shore until you pick up buoys N "4," or even N "6" which mark the eastern edge of the channel. Be careful not to get on the east side of these buoys. Follow the channel past N "8" and N "10" to the next N "2" and the flashing 2.5-second light. This marks the turning point into the Swinomish Channel.

The rest of the run to Deception Pass is easy enough. *Keep a wary eye out for Seal Rocks and favor the right side of the channel at Hope Island Light to avoid the shoal off Ben Ure Spit.*

You now are in the San Juan Islands. Fidalgo, Skagit, Kiket, Strawberry, Ben Ure, Pass, and Deception islands are included in the archipelago. The waters around Hope Island are known for producing some large king salmon.

Tiny **Skagit Island** is usually passed by without a second glance, but in the late 1890's it achieved a measure of questionable fame as a hideout for criminals and smugglers. They also used Skagit Island as a transfer point or temporary storage for their smuggled or stolen goods. Benjamin Ure, for whom **Ben Ure Island** was named, often was host to these shady characters. At one time a wealthy landowner in the Anacortes area and former customs officer, Ben Ure went into the

The town of LaConner on the Swinomish Channel is a popular stopover. Public moorage is at the north end of the town. Cruisers can find fuel, ice, groceries, dining, and shopping.

liquor smuggling business and is said to have provided Canadian spirits for the soldiers at Camp Pickett during the Pig War days on San Juan Island.

It was on Skagit Island, in 1901, that the law finally caught up with Henry Ferguson, alias Wagner, a notorious badman who smuggled, robbed, hijacked ship cargoes, and generally terrorized waterfront and island residents of Puget Sound and the San Juans.

Ben Ure Island lies in **Cornet Bay**, which indents the north end of Whidbey Island just inside Deception Pass. Ben Ure Island can be passed on either side, but on a low tide the western passage is not recommended without local knowledge.

Cornet Bay was named for John Cornet, who lived there in the 1860's. It is popular for an overnight stopover or as a place to await favorable currents for the run through Deception Pass. A state marine park, with floats and mooring buoys, is on the eastern shore. A little farther in is the **Cornet Bay Marina**. Entrance to the marina is through a narrow but well-marked channel.

Pass Island separates the main channel of **Deception Pass** from **Canoe Pass**. While most yachtsmen use the main channel, there are those who like the run through Canoe Pass. Some skippers maintain the current is not as strong there, but I have never verified this. It is an interesting and scenic little pass. *If the current is running, be sure to have some reserve power and keep a close lookout for the rock in the north side of the channel right in the bend, just inside the bridge.*

Deception Pass itself is worrisome to some skippers, while others—mostly those with fast boats—think little about it. Currents on a spring tide run up to 9 knots, creating boils and whirlpools with an occasional overfall. Because of this, most skippers are cautious and prefer to run the pass at or near slack water.

On the other hand, I have a friend who will negotiate the pass with a seven-knot boat at any time, so long as he goes with the current. He says he may be swung around a bit, even in a complete 360-degree turn, but he feels there is no danger. He reports that even though it appears the boat will be dashed against the rock walls, the backwash keeps it off.

My friend may be right, but there is still the possibility of being unable to avoid a large drift log spewed up by a big boil. Consequently, I continue to favor running Deception Pass somewhere near the time of slack water.

There are times when the waters of Rosario Strait can kick up a good fuss. The worst tide rips I have ever seen were off Allan Island. If weather reports indicate heavy winds in the Rosario Strait, or if your time at the pass is not favorable, you may want to consider the **Swinomish Channel route**. The Swinomish Channel provides a protected run as well as an interesting alternative route to the more usual passage.

In running the Swinomish Channel past Goat Island to the Hole in the Wall, it is prudent to pay close attention to the buoys, dolphins, and markers. The Swinomish Channel is like a river and can have some shoaling, but it is some 9 feet in depth and well marked with lights, buoys, and ranges. The yachtsman will want to have a camera ready for some spectacular shots through Hole in the Wall. I also recommend a stop at the old pioneer town of LaConner. Beginning as a trading post in 1867, the town site was sold in 1869 to John S. Conner who named the post office LaConner for his wife, Louise A. Conner.

Some restaurants and shops in LaConner have dock space adjacent.

COLIN HOLME

The orange-painted Rainbow Bridge marks the southern edge of LaConner.

The port's marina offers an excellent moorage while the skipper and crew "do the town." *Watch the current, though, while docking, or entering and leaving a slip. It can run fast and strong in the moorage area and surprise the unwary skipper.*

The north end of the channel entering **Padilla Bay** is through moderately "thin" water for a stretch of a little over 2 miles, so *yachtsmen are well advised to watch the buoys and stay in the middle to avoid any shoaling along the edges.* This route leads to Anacortes and is the gateway to Bellingham and the eastern San Juans.

Not all island visitors come from the Puget Sound and southern ports. Those coming from California, Oregon, or Victoria, B.C. plot their courses via Cattle Pass and San Juan Channel, or via Haro Strait either to **Mosquito Pass** or **Spieden Channel**. From Sidney and vicinity there are several scenic courses through lovely islands that really are a part of the Canadian Gulf Islands complex. From Sidney, the usual route is through the Mosquito Pass or Spieden Channel gateways.

From the north, most skippers come through the Gulf Islands via **Swanson Channel** or **Plumper Sound**. Some, if the weather is right, may run right down the Strait of Georgia to **Boundary Pass**. Northern gateways to the heart of the San Juans include a course that rounds Stuart Island's **Turn Point**, thence to **Spieden Channel**; through **Johns Pass**, the **Cactus Islands**, and **New Channel**; down the west side of **Waldron Island**, or on the east side through **President Channel**.

If all this leaves you with the impression that the San Juan Islands are a center of cruising activity in Northwest waters, you are absolutely right. The islands are not the only such center, of course, for there are many, but certainly the San Juans area ranks high on the list. These "emerald gems set in an inland sea" have been so endowed by a generous nature that they have become the actual or dreamed-of destination for many thousands of boating families. Even the descriptive names given them—such as Treasure Islands of the Northwest, Paradise Isles, Magic Islands, and many more—fail to convey the full measure of their charm.

The San Juan Islands must be experienced to be appreciated. One must cruise or relax among the islands by day, and then, when the sun has set and an open cockpit meal has topped off a perfect day aboard, one must sleep among the islands at night. This prescription for island magic will soothe and heal the vacationing visitor and, in the taking, it will taste good!

Deception Pass

3

FIDALGO ISLAND

Skyline Marina facing Burrows Bay on
Fidalgo Island has guest moorage, fuel,
ice, haulout and repairs.

EDEN ARTS

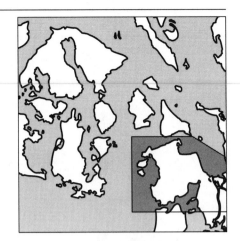

Reservation Bay
Smith Island
Allan Island
Burrows Island
Skyline

It was one of those days of San Juan Islands cruising—or any cruising for that matter—when we "got up before breakfast." Slack current at Deception Pass was at 0705. The Cornet Bay Marina was quiet.

Although the early morning promised another sunny, banana-belt day, the air was crisp and already scented with coffee and frying bacon. Apparently we were not the only ones who intended to make the first slack at the pass.

Following a hearty cruising breakfast, we carefully reviewed the markers on both sides of the channel leading to deep water. We ran the pass without incident, then swung around **Lighthouse Point** and into **Reservation Bay**. Reservation Bay is interesting, but not much used by yachtsmen, although it is an excellent layover to wait for slack on an easterly trip through Deception Pass. *It is a good idea, however, to pay close attention to large-scale chart 18427 to avoid Coffin and Gull rocks.*

Deception Island, lying just outside the entrance to Deception Pass, is not of too much interest to yachtsmen, except as a heading or reference point in approaching the pass from Rosario Strait. The island was named after Deception Pass by the U.S. Coast Survey in 1854. Captain Vancouver named the pass itself Deception Pass because he felt he had been deceived into believing it to be the entrance to a bay. Subsequent investigation proved his error.

Perhaps this is the proper place to log **Smith Island** and **Minor Island**. These two islands are detached from the rest of the archipelago and are of no particular interest to the cruising yachtsman. Still, the Smith Island Light is a most important one in this area. Smith and Minor islands are a sort of halfway marker for the trip across the Strait of Juan de Fuca to or from the San Juans. The two islands are joined at low tide. It is wise not to try to pass between them as a few sailors have done—much to their sorrow—on the Seattle Yacht Club's annual Smith Island Race.

Smith Island and Minor Island were named by the Hudson's Bay Company, but the identity of the person or persons honored seems to be lost. Explorer Eliza called them *Islas de Bonilla* for Antonio de Bonilla, and Wilkes named the larger one Blunt's Island for Simon F. Blunt, his expedition's midshipman.

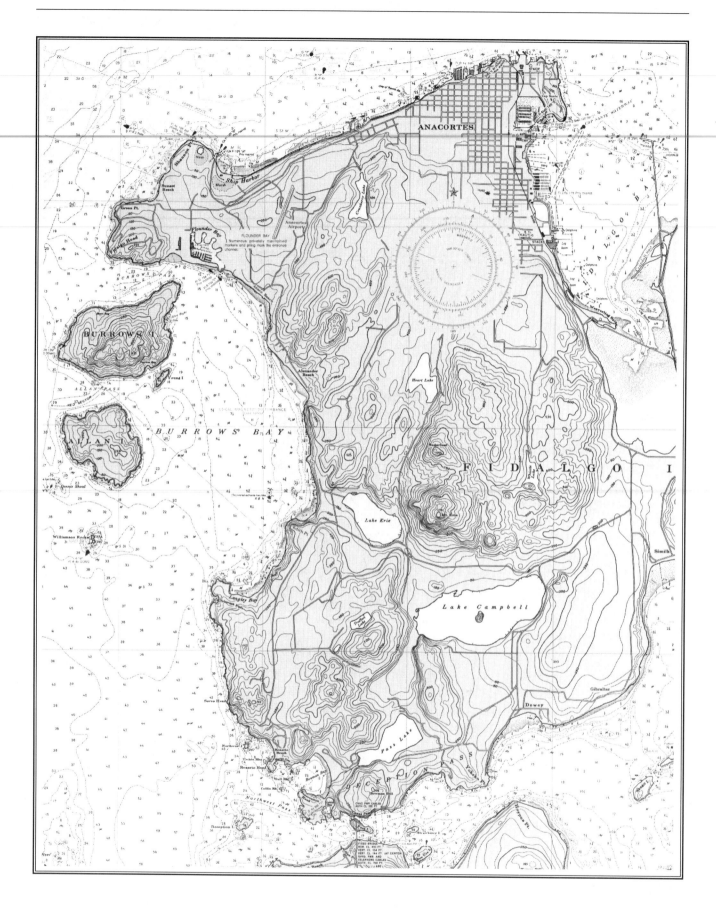

Leaving Reservation Bay, with Skyline Marina as a first destination, we explored **Burrows Bay** and its islands. I have always felt that knowing the source of place-names and something of the local history increased our cruising enjoyment. I had always assumed, for instance, that **Langley Point** and **Langley Bay** on Fidalgo Island at the southern end of Burrows Bay were named for the same man for whom the town of Langley on Whidbey Island was named. Not so; Langley Point and Langley Bay were named for a pioneer settler who lived on the bay behind the point.

Careful piloting is required to enter Reservation Bay, but the cove's scenery makes the effort worthwhile.

The group of rocky islets charted as **Williamson Rocks**, just south of Allan Island, was named by Lieutenant Charles Wilkes for John G. Williamson, one of the expedition's gunners.

Allan Island has a somewhat scalloped shoreline with steep sides. What coves it has are open, except for one on the east side, which offers some protection. Allan Island was named by Wilkes for Captain William Henry Allen, who was killed aboard the *Argus* in the War of 1812. At some point an *a* was substituted for the *e* and so it remains today. Wilkes also called Burrows Bay Argus Bay on his charts.

Wilkes, who was the head of the U.S. Exploring Expedition of 1838-42, was an ardent hero-worshiper, particularly of U.S. naval heroes. During his explorations he named a large number of islands, bays, points, and waterways for these men, even though some of the places already had names. Later, Captain Henry Kellett of the British Admiralty restored many of the original names when he prepared new charts in 1847. Although Wilkes was a great namer of places he explored, his own name does not appear anywhere in the state of Washington.

Burrows Island has a smoother shoreline with fairly steep sides. There are a couple of little bights but best protection is in or near **Peartree Bay** behind **Young Island**. *Be wary of the rock nearly in mid-channel between Burrows Island and Young Island.* The Washington State Parks and Recreation Commission owns 40 acres of land on the western tip of Burrows Island near the lighthouse.

Burrows Island was named by Wilkes for Lieutenant William Burrows, naval hero of the *Hornet*. Wilkes also gave the name Hornets Bay to the body of water we know as Bellingham Bay. He named Young Island for an American fur trapper, Ewing Young.

Skyline, in Flounder Bay, is one of the principal marinas on Fidalgo Island. Skyline has an excellent restaurant, a store, and complete facilities to meet the yachtsman's every need.

Flounder Bay, originally named Boxer Bay for the ship on which Captain Burrows was killed, served as the log pond for an electric sawmill built on pilings over the water during the 1920's. Popular usage changed the name to Flounder Bay, presumably because a large number of flounder were found there before it was dredged.

OPPOSITE PAGE: The west coast of Fidalgo Island, showing Deception Pass, Reservation Bay, and Skyline in Flounder Bay. To transit Deception Pass, skippers should check the current predictions. The easiest passages are made at or near slack water. The flood current flows from west to east through Deception Pass; the ebb current flows from east to west.

Not intended for navigation

Cornet Bay is a good place to spend a night or wait for good current conditions in Deception Pass. Stay in the marked channel.

A view of the Cornet Bay marina. Fuel and ice are available.

The approach to the Cornet Bay marina, showing the channel markers.

The early dredging and filling affected the western 40 acres of Flounder Bay, including the original entry channel. The bay has since been dredged several times to improve navigability. More recently, it was dredged to create a series of moorage basins for private homes. The fill now extends west from the present entry channel to the base of Fidalgo Head and the beginning of the air strip.

The sawmill operation once occupied the entire area at Skyline, from the present restaurant site to the deep water of Burrows Bay.

Lumber was shipped by rail and sea. The extent of the ships' dock can be visualized at low tide by inspecting the piling stubs remaining on the Burrows Bay side of the property. The main mill was demolished in 1961, but the building housing the planing mill, longer than two football fields, was preserved and is now used for dry boat storage. In the lumbering days, some 150 men worked in the mill and there was a hotel, railroad station, and recreation hall.

View of Deception Pass, looking from east to west. Deception Pass connects Fidalgo Island and Whidbey Island. Strawberry Island guards the eastern end of the pass, with Ben Ure Island to the left.

Sunset Beach, in the western part of Anacortes, has a good launch ramp.

The Cap Sante marina has haulouts, repairs, fuel and ice. Well-stocked chandleries are nearby, as well as groceries and shopping in the Anacortes commercial district.

Just west of Skyline, on Fidalgo Head, are **Havekost Park** and monument and **Washington Park**. Tonges H. Havekost was one of the earliest and most civic-minded settlers on the northwestern tip of Fidalgo Island. At the time of his death in 1910, Havekost owned much of the property adjoining Flounder Bay and had bequeathed a portion of the property to the city of Anacortes. He stipulated that the land must be used as a park named for him, and that a monument be erected in his memory.

Anacortes, known as the Gateway to the San Juans, is another of the towns named for a woman. Originally called Ship Harbor, in 1876 the name was changed to Anacortes by town platter and developer Amos Bowman. Bowman used his wife's maiden name of Anna Curtis, giving it a flavor to fit in with Fidalgo and other Spanish names of the area.

Fidalgo Island is connected to the mainland by bridges across the Swinomish Channel (one at the channel's northern end; the other, the Rainbow Bridge, at LaConner), and to Whidbey Island by the Deception Pass Bridge. Thus Anacortes is more of a mainland town than an island town. Anacortes has several attractive and interesting parks, some of them with fine viewing points. Among rock hounds its beaches are known for their jasper, agate, vesuvianite, and serpentine

(known locally as Whidbey Island jade). Principal Anacortes industries are oil refineries, wood, pulp, plywood, and hardboard plants.

As the Gateway to the San Juans, Anacortes has several good marinas and shipyards. Many cruising skippers from Puget Sound points, as well as eastern Washington towns and cities as far away as Los Angeles and Chicago, moor their boats at Anacortes during the summer or even the year-round. This eliminates the long run to Anacortes, and gets boating families to their favorite cruising grounds as much as a day earlier. There are also several good charter services operating in Anacortes.

Anacortes and Fidalgo Island, with the surrounding waters and companion islands, are merely a prelude or *entr'acte* to the cruising paradise of the San Juans. Their water-carpeted passages, generously sprinkled with dancing diamonds by a beneficent summer sun, are the yachtsman's roads and byroads among the many fir, pine, and madrona-clad islands leading to the tranquility of a favorite cove or a rendezvous at a popular resort. Anacortes is merely the beginning of the San Juans journey.

The Cap Sante marina, looking from east to west. The two powerboats approaching the entrance are within the marked channel. Outside the channel the water is shoal.

4

THE EASTERN ISLANDS

The bay on the south side of Saddlebag Island is a good place for crabbing, and a longtime favorite of Northwest yachtsmen.

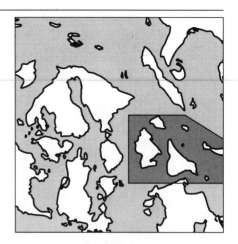

LaConner
Padilla Bay
Saddlebag Island
Guemes Island
Cone Islands
Cypress Island
Strawberry Island

 On one trip, after a stop at LaConner for a visit to that interesting old town, our course took us north through the Swinomish Channel. A flood tide slowed us some but not enough to matter. Many old-time yachtsmen refer to this waterway as Swinomish Slough. I have been told that technically it is not a slough, and that local residents resent the use of the term. Although an old chart in my possession shows "slough" instead of "channel," I shall go along with the sentiments of the residents and call it the Swinomish Channel.

The run between lush farm fields was interesting, but we were kept busy watching for and logging the buoys and lights of the channel into Padilla Bay. The name Padilla Bay comes, as do several names in this area, from the rather lengthy name of Eliza's patron, the Viceroy of Mexico, Señor Don Juan Vicente de Guemes Pacheco Padilla Horcasitas y Aguayo, Conde de Revilla Gigedo.

March Point, at the tip of the eastern cape of Fidalgo Bay, honors Hiram A. March, who became famous for the cauliflower seed he raised in the vicinity in the early 1890's.

Our immediate destination was **Saddlebag Island**, for a mess of crabs. Saddlebag Island has long been a yachtsman's favorite and is a Washington State Marine Park, with five primitive campsites but no drinking water. It has a nice beach for walking. If you drop your crab trap in the right spot in either of the bays on the north or south side of the island, you are almost sure to be rewarded. Keep only the legal size males, however, so the crabs will continue to reproduce. For a leg stretcher, take a hike on the trail across the island.

Saddlebag Island and neighboring **Dot Island** and **Huckleberry Island** were called Porpoise Rocks by Wilkes, after a brig by this name in his expedition. The U.S. Coast and Geodetic Survey later charted the islands individually with the present more descriptive names. Nearby **Hat Island** was charted by Wilkes as Peacock Island for another of his ships but, again, the U.S. Coast and Geodetic Survey people changed the name to conform to its appearance. Hat Island sometimes is confused with another "Hat Island," located in Possession Sound, between the city of Everett and Whidbey Island. This second Hat Island was named **Gedney Island** by Wilkes, and Gedney Island is the proper name — except to many people in Everett.

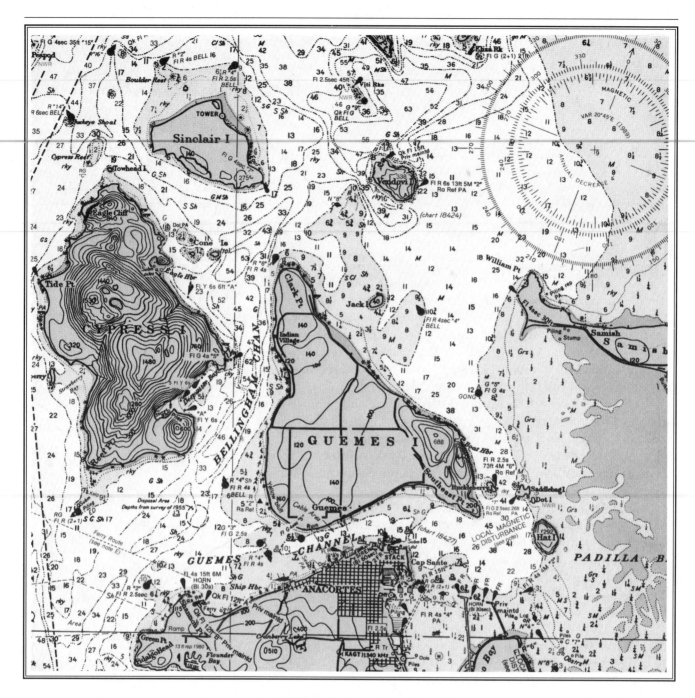

Guemes and Cypress Islands, with smaller islands around them. Note the shoaling in Padilla Bay, east of a line formed by Hat Island, Dot Island, and Saddlebag Island. Considerable eel grass can be found in the vicinity of Hat Island and Saddlebag Island, and sailboat skippers may have to stop and reverse to clear grass from keel and rudder.

Not intended for navigation

Eliza called **Guemes Island** *Isla de Guemes*, part of that long name of the Viceroy of Mexico. Guemes Island is somewhat triangular in shape and has a shoreline practically unbroken by bays or coves. One exception is tiny **Boat Harbor** on the eastern side, about ⅔ of a mile above Huckleberry Island. This little bight is about 100 yards wide and 100 yards long, with 6 feet of depth at zero tide.

A quiet island with both permanent and summer homes, Guemes is served by a ferry from Anacortes which lands at the village of Guemes on the south shore. In the mid-1870's the southwestern corner of the island was home for the notorious smuggler, Lawrence Kelly, and his Indian wife.

Although deep water is found right up to some of Guemes Island's shores, skippers are well advised to be cautious in any beach-combing. *Rocks and kelp are just offshore of Guemes Island in many places. Shoals extend out from Yellow Bluff on the southwest corner, from Clark Point on the northern tip, and from the beach along the northeast shore.*

Guemes Island made newspaper headlines a few years ago when a large company planned to build an aluminum processing plant on the island. County officials, ignoring a comprehensive island plan against such industrial development, welcomed the project, but the storm of protests from local and nearby residents, and from all over western Washington, was so loud that the company cancelled its plans.

Jack Island, located about ¾ of a mile off the northeastern shore of Guemes Island, is privately owned, as is **Towhead Island**, just north of **Cypress Island**. The **Cone Islands**, off the northeast shore of Cypress Island, are a group of five islets and some rocks that bare at low tide. They are scenic and interesting to explore by dinghy. *However, because of rocks and shoals, the Cone Islands should not be approached by large boats without local knowledge.* The two southern islands are owned by the Washington State Parks and Recreation Commission, so you may go ashore.

Probably too many skippers have never noticed, much less investigated, **Samish Island**. Lying a little over 2 miles north of Saddlebag Island, Samish Island is nearly surrounded by shoals and very shallow water, and is actually connected to the mainland. A portion of its 3-mile length was reported to be under consideration as a possible atomic energy site. Although it can hardly be called a bay, the large indentation on the north side behind **William Point** is an excellent crabbing area.

Samish Island was named for the Samish Indian tribe, which lived all along the nearby coastal area. The name comes from an Indian word *samens*, which means hunter.

Lieutenant William Broughton in the *Chatham*, while exploring the San Juan Islands, anchored in **Strawberry Bay** on Cypress Island and named it for the wild strawberries his crew found growing there. Later, Vancouver anchored there and wrote in his journal, "This bay is situated on the west side of an island, which, producing an abundance of upright Cypress, obtained the name of Cypress Island." Although the trees were not cypress, the name has been retained. Eliza, using another of his patron's names, called it *Isla de S. Vincente*.

Vancouver continued, "The Bay is of small extent and not very deep. A small islet, forming nearly the north point of the bay, round which is a clear good passage west; and the bottom of the bay east, at the distance of about three quarters of a mile. This situation, though very commodious, in respect to the shore, is greatly exposed in a SSE direction."

Strawberry Island was named not by Vancouver but by Wilkes, who called it Hautboy. The more common name Strawberry Island is now used on the official charts. Fishing in the bay and around the island is generally good. Strawberry Island was recently purchased by Washington State Department of Natural Resources, as were 680 acres on Cypress Island.

ABOVE AND OPPOSITE: Three views of Saddlebag Island, showing anchorages and especially the shoals to the east.

Cypress Island is rugged, with steep sides in places and with several peaks rising as high as 1,530 feet. There are five lakes on the island, and, in addition to Strawberry Bay, two other harbors. Up near the Cone Islands, **Eagle Harbor** indents the northeast shore, while **Deepwater Bay**, on the southeast side, has its **Secret Harbor**. Both of these harbors are quite shallow: Eagle Harbor with 3 feet and Secret Harbor with 4 feet shallowing to 1 foot, all at zero tide. Courageous skippers with small boats may want to investigate the little bight behind the small peninsula which is the easternmost point of the island. *Caution is advisable, for it, too, has only 1 foot of depth at zero tide and a rock in its entrance.*

While the vast majority of boat owners, after a look at the chart, tend to shy away from places such as these, I have found one of the real joys of cruising to be the cautious exploration of them, and have had many rewarding experiences through the years.

Vendovi Island, which is privately owned, has little to recommend it to the cruising fraternity. It has only one small bay on the northwest end, with a tiny islet in the middle of that bay. Wilkes named Vendovi Island for a cannibal he captured on Viti Levu in the Fiji Islands, while on his way to this area. The expedition's crewmen held Vendovi in contempt and Vendovi, in turn, disdained the local Indians. Vendovi died in a New York hospital after the expedition had returned to the east coast in 1842.

Sinclair Island also has little interest for the yachtsman. It is lower than some of its neighbors, and has both permanent and summer homes. There are some sandy beaches, but no bays or harbors. Both the northwest and northeast sides have shoals and shallow water extending out a fair distance. Shoals extend out to **Boulder Reef** on

34

the northwest, although passage can be made between the reef and the small island if care is used.

Sinclair Island was named by Wilkes for Captain Arthur Sinclair, who commanded the U.S. warship *General Pike* at the beginning of the War of 1812. Sinclair Island has also been known as Cottonwood Island, but is officially shown as Sinclair Island on today's charts.

When Larry Kelly, who was called the King of the Smugglers, was at the height of his notorious career, he bought nearly a section of

land on the northwest side of Sinclair Island. Kelly used the property for a home, farm, and convenient lookout to keep track of the customs boats. Most local citizens of the time did not look upon smugglers as criminals, and, to some degree, even admired them. Kelly was one of those highly regarded by many residents, and was even elected to the school board.

While this group of the eastern San Juan Islands does not offer much in the way of protected harbors, cruising families can find many attractions and points of interest. There are a number of scenic vistas and plenty of opportunities for good photography. There are also good fishing, clamming, and crabbing spots in the area.

C H A P T E R

5

CHUCKANUT AND BELLINGHAM

Village Point with Lummi Peak
in the background.

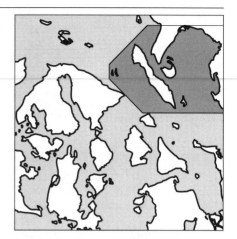

There might be some question as to whether **Chuckanut Island** should be included in the San Juan group. I arbitrarily include it for several reasons. To begin with, technically, Chuckanut Island is within the prescribed limits of Washington Sound. Certainly it is within the eastern cruising section of the San Juans. But, above all, Chuckanut Island should be included, along with the lovely bay behind it, because the island has the same characteristics of beauty and charm found in the rest of the San Juans.

Chuckanut Island is rather like a host or *maitre d'* for beautiful Chuckanut Bay. A tiny islet and a couple of rocks are close off the island's southern end. Otherwise, from the south the entrance to the bay is clear. North of Chuckanut Island, **Chuckanut Rock** and some lesser rocks lie approximately halfway between the island and the northern point of the bay. *There is enough room and depth for entrance on either side of the rocks, but use caution.*

Chuckanut is an Indian word of obscure meaning, but it seems to fit the island. Eliza called the bay *Puerto del Socorro*, meaning "Port of Help." Although the shores are privately owned, there is protected anchorage both in the north end, and in **Pleasant Bay** at the south end, behind **Governors Point**.

It also may seem strange to include **Bellingham** in a cruising guide to the San Juans. I do so because Bellingham is a major center for supplies, facilities, and services for island residents, and is convenient for yachtsmen cruising in the area. The Bellingham Yacht Club, located in Bellingham's excellent Squalicum Small Boat Harbor, is most hospitable to visiting members of other clubs.

While **Bellingham Bay** has ample depth except at its northern end, its waters are still shallow enough for winds to kick up a fair chop. Eliza, the first European to explore the bay, named it *Seno de Gaston* (Gulf of Gaston). When Joseph Whidbey explored it the following year, Captain Vancouver, in charge of Whidbey's expedition, charted it as Bellingham Bay. Vancouver did not state in his journal specifically whom he was honoring, but all evidence favors Sir William Bellingham, controller of the storekeepers' accounts for His Majesty's Navy, and one of the last officials to have contact with Vancouver before Vancouver left England. It is also assumed that Vancouver named

Chuckanut Island
Chuckanut Bay
Bellingham Bay
Portage Bay
Eliza Island
Lummi Island
Hale Passage
Reil Harbor
Inatai Bay
Lego Bay
Barnes Island
Clark Island

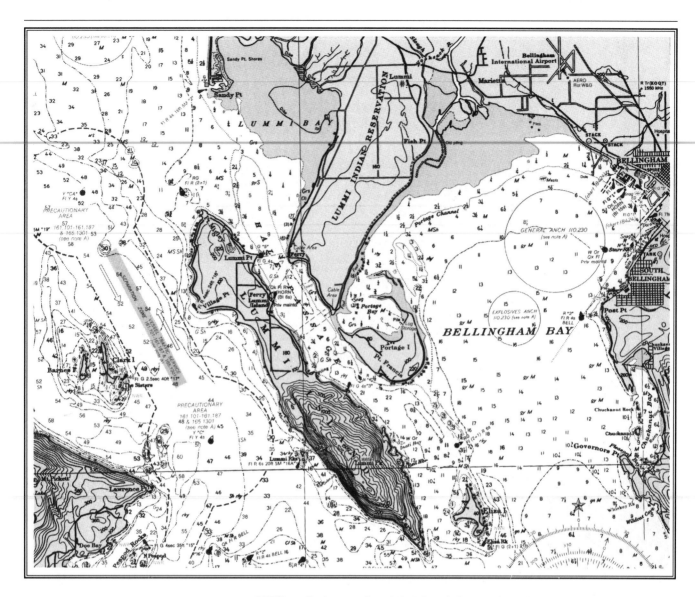

Bellingham Bay, including Lummi Island and Clark and Barnes Islands. Bellingham Bay is larger than it appears on charts. Slower boats are often surprised at the time needed to get from Eliza Island to the small boat harbor. Put the bow on the tall white smokestack in the northeast corner of the bay until the harbor is raised off the starboard bow.

William Point on Samish Island, located at the southern entrance of the bay, for Bellingham.

The Lummi Peninsula, an Indian reservation, forms the northwest boundary of Bellingham Bay. The peninsula's southern tip is almost an island in itself. **Portage Bay**, in the hook, is only for the more adventurous. The bay is shallow and full of rocks and reefs. Vancouver charted the southern tip as **Point Frances**, but his journal does not say for whom the tip was named.

Eliza Island was named for Lieutenant Francisco Eliza, and should be pronounced "Eleeza." It is a beautiful island, almost a suburb of Bellingham, and is well lined with rocks and reefs, particularly on the east side. Eliza Island has two rather open bays with sandy beaches, all privately owned. We enjoyed the most southerly of the two beaches as a lunch-break anchorage on our most recent San Juans cruise.

Eliza Island can deceive the first-time visitor to these waters. If you approach from the south, the low neck of land connecting the western point to the rest of the island makes it appear, at a distance,

LEFT: Just off the south end of Clark Island is a group of rocks called The Sisters.

as two separate islands. So, if you fail to find what appears to be a pair of islands on the chart, don't worry, you aren't lost. The two parts are really one—Eliza.

Lummi Island is a big, interesting piece of land, 7¾ miles long and averaging 1¼ miles wide. Lummi Island's southern half is mountainous, with peaks rising almost vertically from the western shore to Lummi Peak, a height of 1,625 feet. The northern half of Lummi Island is flatter and well wooded. Separated from the peninsula by **Hale Passage**, this section of Lummi Island

PHOTO COURTESY PORT OF BELLINGHAM

ABOVE: Tall pines mark a tip of Barnes Island, which, like Clark Island, lies almost in the middle of Rosario Strait.

LEFT: This spacious launch ramp is located at the south end of Bellingham's Squalicum boat harbor.

is studded with many beach homes. Many of the island's year-round residents commute to their jobs in Bellingham by ferry across Hale Passage.

The points at the two tips of Lummi Island were named by Wilkes for members of his expedition. **Point Migley**, at the north end, was named for Williams Migley, a gunner. **Carter Point**, at the south end, was named for William Carter, a petty officer.

Cruising up the east shore of Lummi Island, one finds **Reil Harbor**. This harbor has little to offer, although it provides some protection from a northwest wind. **Inati Bay**, a bit farther up, provides fair shelter in 4½ fathoms. Farther along are two small bights which could be used in certain winds. Lummi Point, with its sandy beaches, projects far enough into Hale Passage to provide protection on one side or the other, again depending on wind direction.

Hale Passage is a popular San Juans fishing spot and, on a recent visit, we were lucky enough to hook a 12-pound silver salmon there in about 15 minutes of trolling.

The west side of Lummi Island has an almost even shoreline with no good bays or harbors. In **Legoe Bay**, which is entirely exposed to the south, one sometimes sees a fleet of reef net fishing boats.

Passing inside **Lummi Rocks**, the yachtsman finds plenty of room and depth. **Vita Rocks**, southwest of Carter Point, were named by Wilkes for the Fiji Island home of his captive, Vendovi, who was mentioned earlier. Vita Rocks have a light and there is plenty of room between the rocks and the point.

The next heading might be on **Barnes** and **Clark** islands. It is a short crossing, but a strong ebbing current can produce some tide rips along with boiling and swirling waters. **The Sisters** form rocky highrise apartments for the seagulls just off the south end of Clark Island. Especially during mating season, the rocks and the air around them are alive with these gulls. Seals are sighted here on occasion.

The Bellingham and Squalicum boat harbors, located in the northeast corner of Bellingham Bay. Chandleries, a fuel dock, and repairs are available. The Bellingham Yacht Club overlooks the water in the older moorage, behind the breakwater, and is a good place for visitors with reciprocal yacht club privileges to have lunch or dinner.

PHOTO COURTESY PORT OF BELLINGHAM

Both the gulls and the seals make good subjects for the camera bugs. **Clark Island**, the eastern and larger of the two parallel islands, is owned by the Washington State Parks and Recreation Commission. Clark Island has eight primitive campsites, but no drinking water or garbage facilities. It does, however, have beautiful views of other islands. Clark Island has pleasant sand and gravel beaches, and for exploration there are fine places to go ashore in a small boat or dinghy.

Originally, the Spanish named the pair of islands *Islas de Aguayo,* honoring the Viceroy of Mexico. Wilkes renamed Clark Island for Midshipman John Clark, who was killed in Admiral Perry's battle on Lake Erie. Wilkes named **Barnes Island** for an unidentified naval hero. Barnes Island is the site of several private homes.

In cruising between Barnes and Clark islands, be aware of the rocks and reefs off Clark Island's south end and northwest tip, and off the north end of Barnes Island.

The charts are indefinite as to whether these waters are the southern end of the Strait of Georgia or the northern end of Rosario Strait. I am inclined to feel that the Strait of Georgia merges with Rosario Strait about on a line running along Patos, Sucia, and Matia islands, and over to the northern tip of Lummi Island.

The exact identification of the water, however, makes not a bit of difference to yachtsmen cruising in this area. The waters are still a part of this whole charming inland sea, pasturing its herd of lush green islands where the skipper has more choices of channels, passages, bays, and coves than he can use in several boating seasons.

C H A P T E R

6

THE NORTHERN FRINGE ISLANDS

Bruce Calhoun's the *Alldun* and the
Lady Patricia lie at anchor in Shallow Bay,
on the west side of Sucia Island.

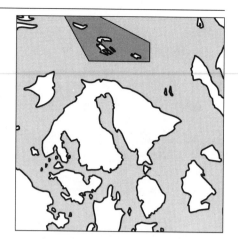

One of the joys of cruising is visiting unfrequented areas often found surprisingly close to the more heavily traveled routes. Such fringe areas in the San Juans include three small islands named Matia, Sucia, and Patos.

Juan Pantoja y Arriaga and his crew on the *Santa Saturnina* were the first Europeans to see Matia, Sucia, and Patos islands. Sent by Eliza to explore the San Juans, Arriaga's party entered Rosario Strait from the Gulf Islands and the Strait of Georgia.

Matia Island (pronounced Mah-tee-ah) was first charted as *Isla de Mata*. It was given the present name, which means "no protection," by the U.S. Coast Survey of 1854. Locally, the island is sometimes called Matey.

The small sister island to the east of Matia Island was named **Puffin Island** in 1858-59 by Captain Richards, after the tufted puffin he found there. This island was renamed Matia East by the U.S. Coast Survey, but the U.S. Coast and Geodetic Survey later changed the name back to Puffin Island.

Matia Island's most prominent early-day resident was a Civil War veteran, Captain Elvin H. Smith, who was known as the Hermit of Matty (Matty being another name for the island). Smith built a comfortable cabin at the head of the southeastern bay. The cabin overlooked Puffin Island, which he called Little Matia, and had a gorgeous view of the surrounding sea and islands.

Captain Smith planted a garden and orchard, raised sheep, rabbits, and chickens, and spread a fish net across the bay's entrance. He made a weekly trip to Orcas Island for mail and staples, first by rowboat, and later powering his boat with an early small outboard motor. Although Captain Smith was called a hermit and was in many ways a solitary person, he was not antisocial. At various times he entertained house guests, including John Vliet, his old war service buddy, Philip Van Buskirk, a navy man, and George Carrier, another friend from war days. Smith also had many friends on Orcas Island.

Life was good in this island paradise, and Captain Smith enjoyed it well into his 80's. In February 1921, however, after being stormbound on Orcas Island for several days, Smith and George Carrier set out for Matia Island from North Beach on Orcas Island. They were in Smith's small boat, which was loaded with supplies.

Matia Island
Puffin Island
Sucia Island
Echo Bay
Fossil Bay
Snoring Bay
Fox Cove
Shallow Bay
Patos Island
Alden Bank
Active Cove

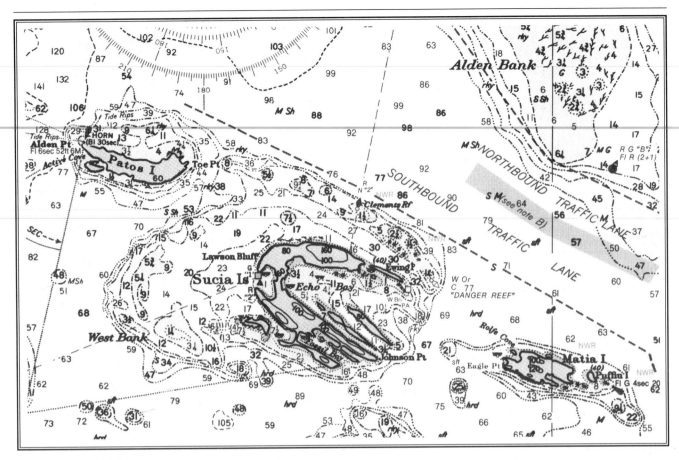

Patos, Sucia, and Matia Islands. Sucia Island is the most
popular, but Matia Island should not be overlooked.

Not intended for navigation

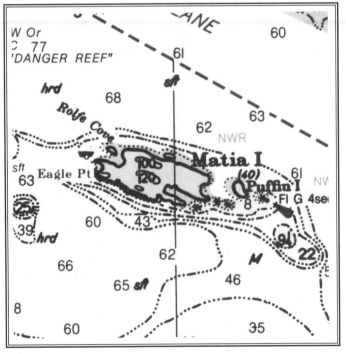

ABOVE: In a pleasant cove on the southeast side of Matia Island, Walt Woodward's *Big Toot II* takes its leisure for an afternoon.

LEFT: Anchorage in a beautiful cove on the western end of Matia Island.

DAVE CALHOUN

ABOVE: Puffin Island lies just east of Matia Island.

LEFT: This dock and float are in the cove at Matia Island's northwest corner. The cove is a marine park, and has good anchorage for a number of boats and a good beach for dinghying ashore.

Walt Woodward and crew explore a rocky shoreline of Matia Island. This photo was taken many years ago, but the activity is timeless.

An aerial view of the west side of Matia Island, showing clearly the two good anchorages.

EDEN ARTS

Winds had abated somewhat, but a good breeze was still blowing from the southeast. The two men failed to make it back to Matia Island and were never found. Part of a wrecked boat with Captain Smith's outboard motor washed up on a distant shore. Today, two empty graves in an Orcas Island cemetery honor these old soldiers.

Today, all yachtsmen can enjoy the lush beauty of Matia Island. Set aside by the government as a bird sanctuary, part of Matia Island also is used as a state marine park, with dock and floats, toilets, and camp and picnic facilities, all located at the bay on the northwest end. Bird lovers will enjoy hikes through the woods and along pebbly or flat-rock shores. Seals usually can be seen sunning themselves on the rocks of Puffin Island, and one might catch sight of a rare sea parrot, hummingbird, or bittern among the more common ducks, shags, seagulls and other seabirds. Matia Island is well endowed with island magic.

EDEN ARTS

Matia Island, looking west. Note the two anchorages. The tip of Puffin Island is in the lower right corner of the photo.

The essence of cruising in the San Juans.
A small cruiser, snug and private,
in Echo Bay at Sucia Island.

Shallow Bay, on the west side of Sucia
Island, offers excellent anchorage.
Other good anchorages are clearly visible.
Sucia is excellent for hiking and exploring.

EDEN ARTS

Fossil Bay, on the southern side of Sucia Island, is a popular anchorage in the summer.

The northern side of Echo Bay provides excellent anchorage in protected coves. From the bay itself these anchorages may look forbidding, but they should be explored and tried.

EDEN ARTS

EDEN ARTS

Top: This view of Sucia Island, looking westward, makes Sucia look almost harsh and forbidding. In reality the dramatic land structures combine to make Sucia Island and its many anchorages an exciting and welcoming destination.

Bottom: The eastern tip of Patos Island, a government-owned island northwest of Sucia Island.

The most heavily visited island in this area is **Sucia Island**, somewhat better known to cruising families than Matia Island. Sucia Island really is a troop of at least 11 islands and islets, but the cluster is commonly referred to in the singular. Sucia Island itself is horseshoe shaped, encircling lovely **Echo Bay**. **Ewing Island**, off the northeastern tip, completes the horseshoe, with four smaller islets lying close inside. On the southern side of Echo Bay are **Northern Finger Island**, and, lying parallel, the two **Southern Finger Islands**. There is plenty of depth on all sides of these long, narrow islands, and rocks are marked by kelp. There is good anchorage in the bay, but *one should avoid getting too close to shore at the head of Echo Bay, where flat rocks can hang boatmen up at low tide.* If you are not familiar with the area, it is best to take soundings within the scope of your swing to be sure you have enough depth when the tide ebbs.

Fossil Bay, indenting the southern part of Sucia Island from the southeast, contains **Herndon Island**, where Captain Chris Wilkins lived, and which he called Christmas Island. Behind is **Mud Bay**, which dries at low tide. Around the point that forms the northern entrance to Fossil Bay is a cove that state park officials dubbed **Snoring Bay** when they found a ranger sound asleep there on his boat.

Little Sucia Island lies off the southwest shore of the big island, near the mouth of a small bay known locally as **Fox Cove**. Two points of land at the front, or western, part of the horseshoe form **Shallow Bay**.

Eliza charted these islands as *Isla Sucia*. In Spanish nautical parlance, *sucia* means "dirty" or "foul" because of hidden rocks. The name referred to the many rocks and reefs in the waters around the islands. Despite its meaning, the name has a pleasing sound and is appropriate for these beautiful islands. Wilkes called the islands the Percival Group, honoring Captain John Percival, but in 1847 Kellet restored the name Sucia.

If one discounts early-day smuggling and rum running, Sucia Island has been a quiet place until recent years. During the 1890's, the government was asked to open the island to homesteading, which was answered with the announcement that it was being reserved for coastal defense. A military post was never built, however.

Sandstone was quarried on Sucia Island, and in the early 1900's the streets of several Puget Sound towns, including Seattle, were paved with sandstone bricks from there. Some years later Captain William Hernden operated an excursion boat, the *Tulip King*, through the islands. Hernden lived with his family on Sucia Island for a number of years, until he moved to Orcas Island after his home burned during the 1930's.

In the late 1950's, when Sucia Island was about to be sold for private development, Ev G. Henry, a leading Northwest yachtsman and "father-founder" of several Northwest boating organizations, rallied the forces of the Puget Sound Interclub Association to save the island for yachtsmen. Under Ev Henry's guidance and leadership, individuals in the member yacht clubs and boating organizations assessed themselves two dollars a year each for a period of three years. A specially negotiated purchase price was met and Sucia Island was acquired. It was turned over to the Washington State Parks and Recreation Commission to become the fine marine park that it is today.

The Interclub Association worked with commission officials to have the point forming the southern side of Fossil Bay named **Ev Henry Point**, as a lasting tribute to the man who engineered the saving of Sucia Island for the boating public. A memorial plaque is located in front of a large sign that lists the yacht clubs that helped acquire Sucia Island for a state marine park.

In Fossil Bay you will find two docks and floats, and mooring buoys. Water is available, as are camp and picnic sites with stoves, toilets, and garbage pickup ashore. Interesting fossils may be found and dug from the rocky banks of the bay's south shore, and

clams, oysters, and crabs are abundant. Trails lead to Fox Cove, Echo Bay, and across the low, narrow strip from Echo Bay to Shallow Bay, with its gently sloping gravel beach and quiet seclusion. A spectacular shore of eroded sandstone columns and caves marks the place where smugglers are supposed to have cached their contraband silk, wool, opium, and whiskey from across the border. Another trail leads out to the northeast point, offering a host of fascinating things to see.

BELOW AND OPPOSITE: Two views of Fox Cove, showing little Sucia Island (below), and anchorages in Fossil Bay.

Cruising families will enjoy going ashore for exploration and a chance to stretch their legs. Do not forget to take the camera with you on these hikes.

Swimming can be good from the sandy beaches of Sucia Island's bays. Usually, the water is warmer than elsewhere in the San Juans. Exploring the shallower reaches of the bays by dinghy is another

EDEN ARTS

pastime, and jigging for cod in the kelp beds off the northeast point can be rewarding.

In approaching **Shallow Bay**, do not be misled by what appears to be a solid line of kelp across the entrance between the two points. A reef and a rock extend southerly from the north point. ***Take it slow, favor the south point a bit, and a break in the kelp will open up.*** While, as the name implies, the water is shallow, it averages around 2 fathoms at zero tide. Choose your anchorage behind one of the points according to the wind direction, or predicted direction, of northwesterly, westerly, or southwesterly.

With so much to see, do, and enjoy on Sucia Island, it is no wonder it has become a favorite with many boating families who

return again and again to partake of its solitude, primitive charm, and many other attributes.

Patos Island, about 1½ miles northwest of Sucia Island, might be called the northern outpost of the San Juans. Here is another island that has undergone some name changes. The Spaniards Galiano and Valdes in 1792 called it *Patos*, meaning "ducks" in Spanish. In his spree of assigning new names, Wilkes changed the name to Gourd Island, presumably because of its shape. Captain Kellett did not approve of the change, and in 1847 restored the original name of Patos Island.

Both **Alden Point**, at the western tip of Patos Island, and **Alden Bank**, an extensive reef to the east of the island, were named for Lieutenant Commander James Alden. Alden served in this area with

Wilkes, and later commanded the steamer *Active* in hydrographic surveying of these waters. The descriptive name **Toe Point**, for the point on the eastern end of Patos Island, appeared on British charts in 1888.

Active Cove, a narrow, small bay formed below Alden Point by Little Patos Island, was probably named for Alden's ship, although I have not been able to verify this. *Entrance to Active Cove should not be attempted at the east end of Little Patos Island.* The Patos Island Light, established on Alden Point in 1893, is an important automated light, guiding mariners in Boundary Pass and the southern part of the Strait of Georgia.

Patos Island is a state marine park, with buoys in Active Cove, and four primitive campsites with no water available. Helene Glidden's book, *Light on the Island*, published in 1951, and, unfortunately, now out of print, relates many exciting events that happened on the island when her father was a keeper at the lighthouse there. The island was also used by old-time smugglers as a transfer point. Later, Active Cove was a hideout for customs boats looking for smugglers.

While Patos Island does not have as much to offer the yachtsman as some of the other islands, the short trip is worth the effort. Fishing in the area is above average, with both salmon and cod awaiting the lure. For visitors interested in marine life, depressions in the rocks offshore become aquariums at low tide. They provide an opportunity to study the creatures temporarily imprisoned, or to gather specimens for a biology class. The northern shore is rocky, and an excellent place for driftwood hunters. The southern side features sandy or pebbly beaches between the rocks.

We hear much these days about fringe benefits. Certainly these exotic islands, forming the northern fringe of the San Juans, offer benefits far beyond expectations. The islands are not civilized, are not developed, and offer few modern facilities. Their magic consists of calm serenity, spectacular scenery, and a natural unspoiled setting, all awaiting the vacationing family.

C H A P T E R

7

THE NORTHWEST ISLANDS

Reid Harbor, on the southwestern shore of Stuart Island. Reid Harbor is virtually landlocked, and some 400 yards wide. Good anchorage can be found anywhere in its wider portion. Mooring buoys and mooring floats also are available.

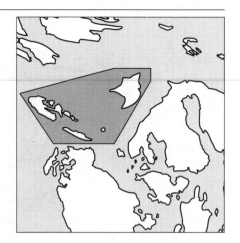

Leaving Sucia Island's Shallow Bay and picking one's way through the "gate" in the kelp hedge across the entrance, *it is wise to keep a close eye on the depth sounder until the West Bank shoal has been cleared.* It is only about 4 miles across the top of President Channel to Waldron Island. However, some skippers may want to alter the course for a closer look at Skipjack Island and Bare Island.

Skipjack Island is approximately 600 yards (³⁄₁₀ of a mile) long, well wooded, and rising to about 120 feet. **Bare Island**, as its name implies, is a big rock. *There are rocks between Skipjack Island and Bare Island, and kelp around Skipjack Island's north shore, so explore with caution.*

Small and minor, Skipjack and Bare islands have had a difficult time establishing their names. Wilkes called them Ship Jack Islands, shipjacks being the common name for a fish caught in the area. In 1853 the U.S. Coast Survey named the islands according to their contrasting appearances, so they became Wooded and Bare islands. Five years later Bare Island was changed to Penguin Island, but later the present names of Skipjack Island and Bare Island appeared on official charts.

Just to the south lies **Waldron Island**, with some interesting history but with little to attract the yachtsman. Two charted bays, **North Bay** and **Cowlitz Bay**, offer very little protection. **Mouatt Reef** sits in the front yard of Cowlitz Bay, where the Waldron dock is located. Mail Bay, a tiny indent on the eastern side of the island, was so named because it was the landing spot for Colonel Enoch May, who, in his old canoe, paddled the mail across from West Beach on Orcas Island in the 1870's. Colonel May not only braved the sometimes wild waters of President Channel, but he also had to scale the steep cliffs around the bay and then walk several miles to the post office. Today the mail boat lands at the county dock at Cowlitz Bay.

There is some question about the source of Waldron Island's name. Some authorities claim the island was named for Thomas W. Waldron, captain's clerk on the *Porpoise*, one of the ships in Wilkes's expedition. Others believe that it was named for R. R. Waldron, purser aboard the *Vincennes*, another member of the Wilkes group. There are also those who believe that the intention was to honor both men.

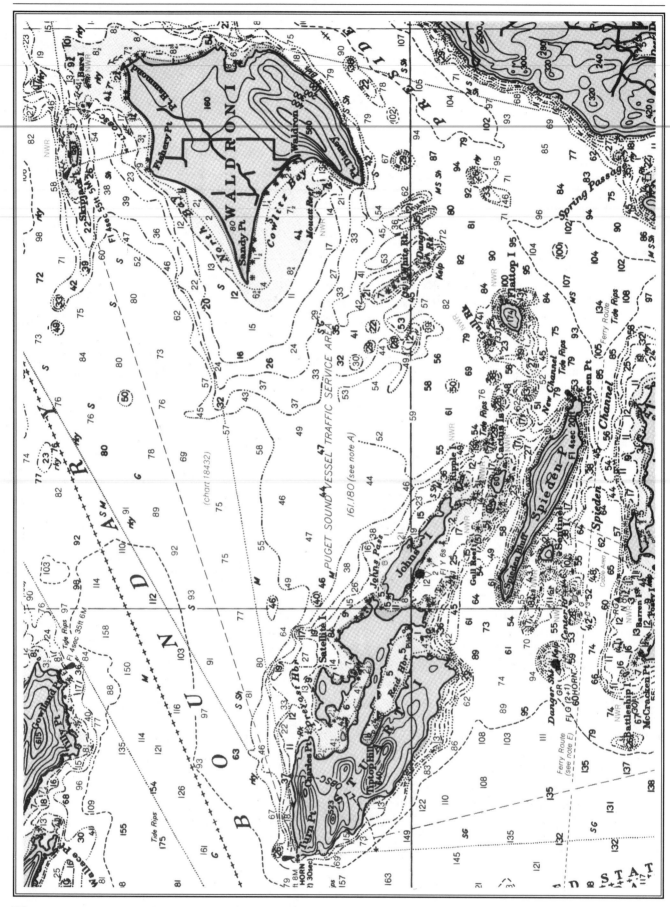

Sentinal Island, to the left in this picture, hovers close to Speiden Island, to the right.

Point Hammond, at the northern tip of Waldron Island, was named by Wilkes for Henry Hammond, one of Wilkes's quartermasters. **Point Disney**, at the southern tip, was named for Solomon Disney, a sailmaker's mate on one of Wilkes's ships.

Waldron Island's sandstone quarries, like Sucia's, provided stones for street paving in Seattle, Tacoma, and other Puget Sound cities and towns shortly after the turn of the century. Possibly because it lacks a good protected harbor, Waldron Island has always been, and still is, a quiet, rural place with few modern developments. Besides stone quarrying, its residents engaged in fishing, farming, logging, and, reputedly, some bootlegging during Prohibition. For the most part, however, the principal occupation is enjoying life. In later years, Waldron Island has attracted writers and artists.

A short distance southwest of Waldron Island are **White Rock** and **Danger Rock**. Danger Rock is owned by the Washington State Parks and Recreation Commission.

Still farther to the southwest, **Flattop Island** and its satellite, **Gull Rock**, are the outposts for a collection of small islands, islets, rocks, and reefs that provide some fascinating exploration possibilities for the more adventuresome. The descriptive name of Flattop was given to the island by Wilkes because of its terrain. The **Cactus Islands, Gull Reef**, and **Ripple Island**, with their scenic attractions and low, level, rocky beaches and photographic possibilities, are fun to investigate. However, the skipper should let someone else take the pictures while he keeps a careful eye on the chart, the depth sounder, and the water around him. Large-scale chart 18432 makes such exploration easier, safer, and more fun. *Watch out for unexpected currents through here, too.*

Just to the south, **Spieden Island** stretches its 2½-mile length to form the northern side of **Spieden Channel**. Named in 1841 by either Wilkes or Ringgold for William Spieden, the purser of the *Peacock*, the name probably should be pronounced "Spee-duhn," but almost everyone calls it "Speye-duhn." In 1970 the island was bought by the Spieden Island Development Corporation. The name was changed to Safari Island and it became a private commercial big-game hunting preserve, stocked with exotic animals and birds brought from their habitats around the world.

OPPOSITE: The northwest islands. Reid Harbor and Prevost Harbor on Stuart Island are popular anchorages and well protected.

Not intended for navigation.

EDEN ARTS

TOP: The Turn Point lighthouse, located on the rocky northern tip of Stuart Island. It's a pleasant walk from either Prevost Harbor or Reid Harbor to the lighthouse.

BOTTOM: Looking northwest across Ripple Island, with Johns Island in the background.

There was considerable controversy about the safari operation. For a rather substantial fee one could hunt, under supervision of a guide, for such rare trophies as Barbary or mouflon sheep, swift India blackbucks, Japanese Sitka deer, Indian spotted deer, European fallow deer, and other wild game. Reports are lacking on the commercial success of the operation, but it folded in 1973. Among the yachting fraternity as well as on the official charts, the island is still called Spieden Island.

Spieden Island was the home of several early San Juans pioneers who made history in these parts. Probably, the best known was Ed "Dad" Chevalier, the "King of Spieden Island." One of nine children of a Dakota plains farmer who had moved west, Chevalier, his brothers, sisters, and his own children played important parts in San Juan Islands affairs through the years.

The Chevaliers were a hard-working family, with their own horses, cows, and sheep. They had a large garden, raised turkeys, cut wood, and logged. Ed Chevalier rowed two miles over and back every day to a job at Roche Harbor, and he built boats for his neighbors. He also did some commercial fishing, and is credited with establishing reef net fishing in the islands. The oldest son, William, rowed two miles each day to the school at the head of Stuart Island's Reid Harbor.

For some years before it became a private hunting preserve, Spieden Island was owned by Seattle industrialist Tony Sulak. Sulak had a comfortable home on top of the island, an aircraft landing strip, and a small boat and seaplane harbor in the little bay behind Green Point at the eastern end.

Sentinel Island, nestled along the southern shore of Spieden Island toward the western end, appears to guard the approach to the larger island. The two islands even look alike because Sentinel Island has the same characteristics as Spieden Island—a wooded north side and a barren south side—making it appear, viewed from the east or

west, like a person's head with the hair clipped closely on just one side.

It was in 1919 that another couple wanting "to get away from it all" claimed Sentinel Island as a homestead. Farrar Burn, brother of old-time radio star Bob Burn, set up housekeeping in a tent with his wife, June. "Dad" Chevalier was their guardian angel, insisting that they move to Spieden Island for their first winter, rescuing them from tenderfoot errors and teaching them the ways of the islands.

June Burn's book, *Living High*, is a delightful account of those days. In 1946, she wrote a daily column titled "100 Days in the San Juans" in the Seattle *Post-Intelligencer*. The column described the Burns' adventures as they sailed and rowed their small boat all through the islands, camping on the beaches, visiting with friends, and enjoying the magic of the area, much as boating families do today. The Burns later lived on Waldron Island.

Thus far, research has failed to disclose who John or Johns was, but, whoever he was, John (or Johns) had an island named for him.

The dock at Reid Harbor has room for several boats at a time. Dinghies from anchored boats can be tied at the ends.

BELOW, LEFT AND RIGHT: These floats in Reid Harbor were filled on summer weekends 20 years ago, and remain popular today.

Johns Island lies east of **Stuart Island**, separated from Stuart Island by scenic **Johns Pass**. We have heard on a few occasions of skippers who were worried about running this pass. The concerns are unnecessary. While care should be taken on the trip, there is no valid reason why the pass should not be used and enjoyed by boatmen.

Johns Pass has depths of 4 to 11 fathoms in mid-channel, a minimum width of about 200 yards, and rocks well marked by kelp. Currents can run up to 5 knots on full tides. *In approaching Johns Pass from the south or leaving from the north, care should be taken to avoid the rocks and shoal extending from Stuart Island's eastern tip, and the foul area extending eastward from Gull Reef.* It should be remembered that a strong flood current can set eastward through here, so allowance should be made for it. Study of the top of chart 18432 can be helpful.

The name Paul K. Hubbs probably turns up more often in San Juan Islands history than any other single name. Originally a southerner, Hubbs lived on San Juan Island and played an active part in political, civil, and military events throughout the Pig War boundary dispute days. Following a heart attack and a doctor's order to move to a town where medical care was available, Hubbs decided that city life and its tensions were the cause of heart trouble, not the cure for it, so he adopted the life and ways of the Indians.

With any of an unknown number of wives he acquired in his wanderings, Hubbs led a nomadic life for another 38 years, his name appearing in the annals of various of the islands including Orcas,

Looking southward at Prevost Harbor on the left and Reid Harbor on the right. Both are well-protected.

EDEN ARTS

Lopez, and Blakely. It was on Johns Island that Hubbs probably had his longest residence. With his current klootchman (Indian wife or mistress), he lived in a crude shack, raised a garden, kept a few sheep, dug clams, fished, and enjoyed his declining years. We shall hear of Paul Hubbs again in this book. Today there are several private homes on Johns Island, with their residents enjoying the life there.

Stuart Island is the northwesternmost of the San Juans group. It is one of the loveliest, with much to offer the cruising family. **Reid Harbor** and **Prevost Harbor**, two majestic landlocked harbors on either side of the island's narrow spine, provide excellent moorage and anchorages. State marine parks in both harbors have many facilities, including camps and picnic sites, toilets, docks, floats, and mooring buoys. Fishing is good on both the north and south sides of

Looking southeast across Reid Harbor and Prevost Harbor. The number of boats show the popularity of the two anchorages.

EDEN ARTS

TOP: Bruce Calhoun's *Alldun* shares a mooring buoy with another cruiser in Reid Harbor.

BOTTOM: This handsome express cruiser is anchored in Prevost Harbor, Stuart Island's other major harbor and also a state marine park.

Stuart Island, and there are clams and oysters for the taking.

Reid Harbor, the southern of the two harbors, is only 3 miles from San Juan Island's Roche Harbor. Reid Harbor is approximately 1½ miles long and averages ³⁄₁₀ of a mile wide, with depths from 1½ to 5 fathoms over a soft bottom. **Gossip Island** and **Cemetery Island**, both owned by the Washington State Parks and Recreation Commission, extend nearly to the middle of the entrance on the starboard hand when entering. *There is also a rock and shoal on the port hand, well marked by kelp, so when entering Reid Harbor a slightly left of center channel course should be held.* Once inside, Reid Harbor is free of any dangers. A trail connects the floats of the state parks on the two harbors.

Prevost Harbor, on the north side of Stuart Island, is a large bay protected by **Satellite Island**. The entrance is between **Charles Point** and the west end of Satellite Island, with kelp-marked shoals on both sides calling for a mid-channel course. *Entrance should not be attempted on the east side of Satellite Island, as it is strewn with dangerous rocks and reefs.*

Prevost Harbor is an excellent shelter and anchorage, a favorite of many cruising families. While there is limited moorage at the state park's floats, good anchorage can be found anyplace in the harbor, with many preferring the little bight near Satellite Island's western end. A rock that dries at 8 feet lies in the entrance to this bight. It is easily located by its kelp covering, but care should be taken to avoid it by favoring either of the outer points of the cove.

Prevost Harbor is a good place to explore by dinghy, to dig for clams, or gather oysters. If sea legs need stretching, it is only a one-mile hike on a trail that runs from the old settlement of Prevost just inside Charles Point, across the north end of the island to the Turn Point Lighthouse. At **Turn Point**, in addition to inspecting the light, one can enjoy a sweeping view of the Canadian Gulf Islands. The scene is spectacular as the sun sets behind Vancouver Island.

Some question surrounds the naming of Stuart Island, with the answer depending on whether one accepts the claims of American or British authorities. Some sources credit Wilkes with naming it, in 1841, for Frederick D. Stuart, a captain's clerk in Wilkes's expedition. Others say it was named by Captain Richards in 1858-59 for Captain Charles Edward Stuart of the Hudson's Bay Company, who was on loan to Commander James Charles Prevost of HMS *Satellite* because of his knowledge of local waters.

Prevost Harbor was named for Commander Charles Prevost, as was Charles Point. Satellite Island takes its name from Prevost's ship, which played a part in the San Juan boundary dispute. Satellite Island was first called James Island by Richards, probably for Commander Prevost. Later the name was changed, perhaps to avoid confusion with James Island in Rosario Strait. Richards also named Reid Harbor, presumably for Captain James Murray Reid of the Hudson's Bay Company.

Stuart Island played its part in the history of the islands with several pioneers, fishermen, and farmers making their homes there. It was also the boyhood home of Ed ("King of Spieden Island") Chevalier. Indians once lived on the point where the Turn Point Lighthouse is located. Shortly after arriving from Norway, Eric and Marie Erickson established their home at Prevost Harbor. Marie was appointed postmistress, a position she held for more than 30 years. At first the mail was distributed from the kitchen of her home; an official post office was established sometime later.

Stuart Island is truly one of the most delightful of the San Juans. With its many attractions, scenic setting, interesting things to do, and rich past, it rates a high priority on a list of favorites with cruising families and should be a part of any San Juan Islands cruising itinerary.

A good dock and other facilities make Prevost Harbor an inviting stop. Across the narrow spine of Stuart Island is Reid Harbor.

8

ORCAS ISLAND

Deer Harbor on Orcas Island, looking southeast.
In the distance is Pole Pass, and the Deer Harbor
Marina is on the east shore.

EDEN ARTS

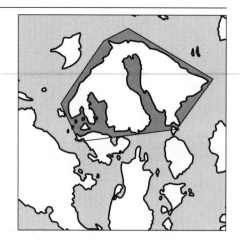

It has been said that in America few places remain where history has not been paved over. In the San Juan Islands, I am happy to report, there has been very little paving over of history. Since the days of Captain Vancouver's explorations, man has become ever more aware of the enjoyment to be found in cruising this tranquil archipelago and the value of preserving its natural wonder.

Orcas Island is no exception. Much of Orcas Island looks as it did to Lieutenant Broughton nearly 200 years ago. Today's residents are doing all they can to keep it that way, and to preserve the mementos and memories of its history. Orcas Island is a sparkling jewel in the crown of this fleet of islands.

Although there are conflicting statements regarding the source of Orcas Island's name, it seems fairly well established that it was Eliza who charted a portion of what we know as San Juan Channel as *Boca de Horcasitas* (after a Spanish ship by that name with the *H* frequently dropped). The name Orcas was given to the island by Captain Kellett in 1847. Some claims are made that the name is derived from *orca*, the Spanish word for killer whale.

As we have pointed out, Wilkes did a lot of name-dropping in this area, but some of the names he bestowed have not been retained, for which we can be thankful. The Spanish names such as Lopez, Sucia, San Juan and others are much more musical and more fitting than those Wilkes used.

A man with a deep love and respect for the navy, Wilkes naturally wished to honor the service and its heroes. He called the entire group of islands the Navy Archipelago. Orcas Island he named Hull's Island for Commodore Isaac Hull, who commanded the *Constitution* in the capture of the English ship *Guerriere*. Old Ironsides Inlet was his name for East Sound, and Guerriere Bay for West Sound. Wilkes' naming of Mt. Constitution has endured.

Orcas Island, with an area of 57 square miles, is the largest of the San Juan Islands, but just barely (nosing out San Juan Island by one square mile). Shaped like a pair of saddlebags, Orcas Island measures 11½ miles east and west and 7½ miles north and south, and has about 70 miles of shoreline. A circumnavigation of the island is a worthwhile project for the cruising yachtsman, but the plan should allow more

West Beach
Freeman Island
North Beach
Parker Reef
Pt. Lawrence
Peapod Rocks
Doe Island
Obstruction Pass
Peavine Pass
East Sound
Eastsound
Grindstone Harbor
Orcas
West Sound
Pole Pass
Deer Harbor
North Pass

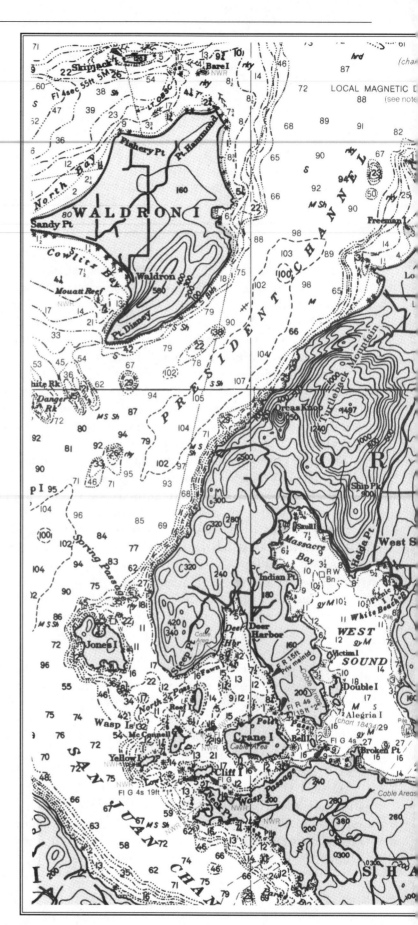

Orcas Island. East Sound, West Sound, and Deer Harbor offer good anchorages, and the watchful skipper can find many others around the perimeter.

Not intended for navigation.

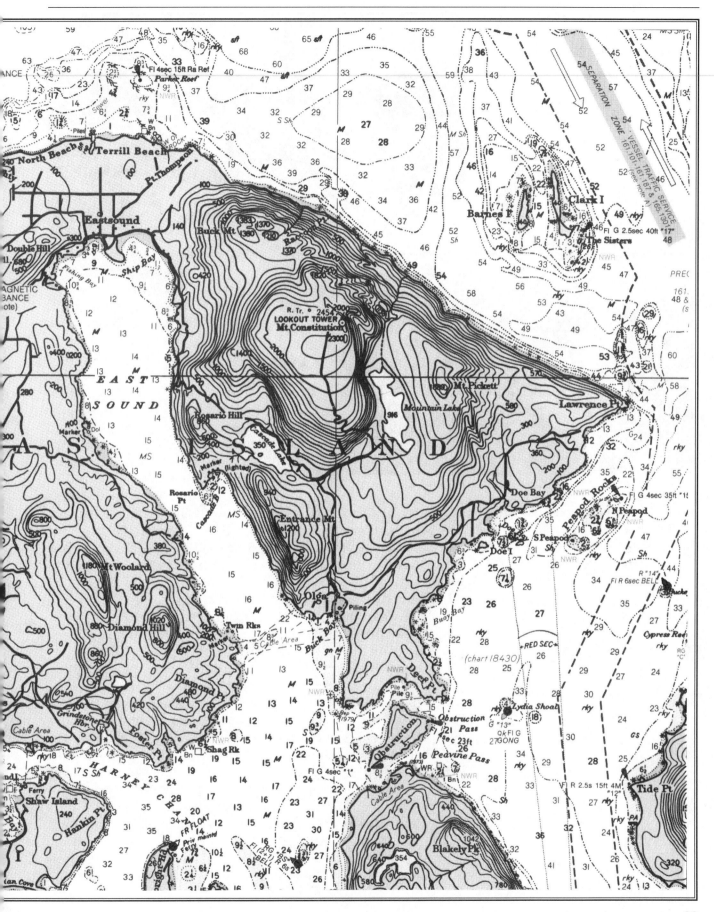

The village of Olga, in Buck Bay near the entrance to East Sound, has a dock and a convenient store.

DAVE CALHOUN

The Orcas landing seen from water level. The sign for the fuel dock can barely be seen above the small house on the dock to left of the ferry dock, and the grocery store can be seen at the head of the ferry dock.

than one day for the trip, as there are many places to visit, explore, or drop the hook for a night's stay.

A circle tour might be made clockwise, starting at **Steep Point**, at the southwest tip of Orcas Island. One can almost beachcomb along the west coast. A few rocks lie close in to the shore, but they are well marked with kelp. **West Beach Resort**, about two-thirds of the way up this coast, offers gas, moorage, groceries, ice, bait, scuba air, propane, laundry, and restrooms. The mooring buoys are owned by the resort. The fishing is exceptional north and south of the resort. Just beyond, **Freeman Island** lies a short distance off the shore. Freeman Island is owned by the U.S. Fish and Wildlife Service, so you may go ashore there. Anchor between Freeman Island and Orcas Island and row in. Freeman Island was named by Wilkes for J. D. Freeman, a sailmaker aboard the *Peacock*.

Below **Point Doughty**, at the northwestern tip of the island, is the YMCA's Camp Orkila. Wilkes named the point for John Doughty, a petty officer on the *Peacock*.

Around the point and along the north shore, beachcombing ceases to be a good idea. Shallow water, shoals, some rocks and acres of kelp discourage it. There are several resorts along the north shore. Smuggler's Villa, a new condominium development with boating facilities for owners but no transient moorage, has been built. The **Captain James Cook Resort** (formerly Bartel's), offers fuel, groceries, ice, lodging, and a boat ramp. Fishing is generally good off **North Beach**, particularly around **Parker Reef**, which Wilkes named for George Parker, one of his petty officers.

Wilkes named **Point Thompson**, marking the end of North Beach, for Matthew Thompson, captain of the top in one of the expedition's crews. The shore is steep and almost straight as it runs northeast from Point Thompson, rising up to Mt. Constitution and

 *credited in margin:* DAVE CALHOUN

The Olga store is near
the head of the dock in Olga.

Mt. Pickett. With the exception of a couple close-in rocks, there are no hazards. The water is deep almost to the shore, so beachcombing may be resumed. In contrast to the western shore, the north shore is rugged, seemingly designed by nature to protect the island from any storms that might blow down from the Strait of Georgia.

Point Lawrence, at the eastern tip of Orcas Island, is considered to be one of the best fishing spots around the island, and carries a famous name that many people may not recognize. Wilkes named the point for James Lawrence, whose dying words, "Don't give up the ship," are a U.S. Navy motto. Lawrence also served aboard the *Constitution* and was commander of the *Wasp*, the *Hornet*, the *Argus*, and the *Vixen*.

The southeast shore of Orcas Island, from Point Lawrence to **Deer Point** at the entrance to Obstruction Pass, changes again to a more scalloped pattern. **Peapod Rocks**, lying off to the southeast, are a state park underwater recreation area and a favorite place for scuba divers. The rocks themselves, however, are a national wildlife preserve so you may not go ashore, but the seals make for good photographic possibilities. *There are strong underwater currents around Peapod Rocks, so divers should be cautious.* Several small bays indent the shore, and **Doe Island** is a 6½-acre state marine park. It offers a small dock and float, picnic tables, five campsites, and pit toilets. There is no fresh water and no garbage pickup, so be prepared.

It was along this shore that Lieutenant Broughton had trouble in the *Chatham*, after exploring in the middle of the islands. On May 21, after Broughton had come through one of the two passes (probably Obstruction Pass), a southeast wind and strong tide set him close to the rocks on the southeast shore of Orcas Island. The small boats

PHOTO COURTESY JAMES F. WILSON/NORTHWEST AIR PHOTOS

Orcas Island is centered in a constellation of smaller islands. Swinging in an arc from upper left are Waldron Island, Patos Island, Sucia Island, and Matia Island. At the lower left of the photo is Jones Island, lying west of Steep Point. The Wasp Islands, lower center, lie in the western approach to West Sound.

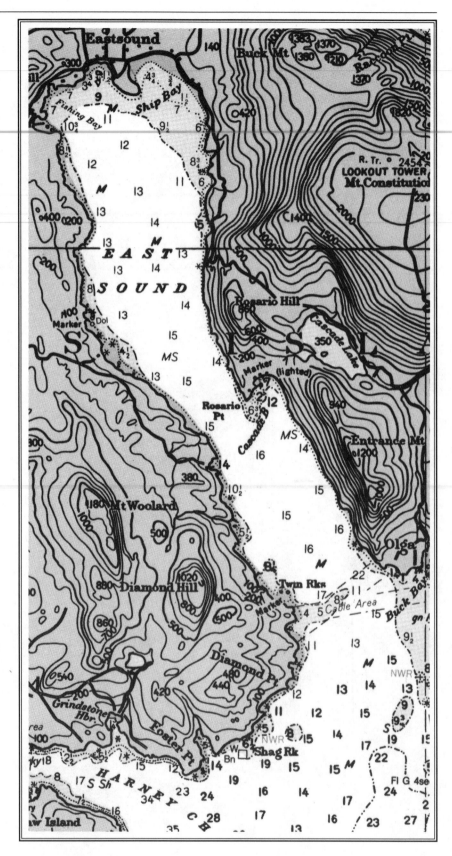

East Sound. Rosario is a popular stopping point, and anchorage can be found in Fishing Bay, at the town of Eastsound.

Not intended for navigation.

were called upon to tow the *Chatham* out of danger. During the operation the *Chatham's* bow touched a rock.

Crewmen were surprised that they could touch a rocky shore on one side of the ship while the sounding showed 22 fathoms on the other side. The sounding continued, and the lead line fouled and broke. As already mentioned, the lead is no doubt still there among the rocks, waiting for some scuba diver to pick it up as a valuable souvenir.

Obstruction Island, lying between Orcas Island and Blakely Island, separates the dogleg-shaped **Obstruction Pass** to the north, and shorter **Peavine Pass** to the south.

Currents can run up to 5 knots through these passes, but usually they are not strong enough to bother most boats. **Lieber Haven Marina Resort** has a small grocery, moorage, boat rentals, and lodging, either in cabins on the beach or on board a 100-foot sea-going tug.

Coming out of Obstruction Pass, one can enter **East Sound**, and swing into **Buck Bay** for a visit to the village of **Olga**. Olga was named for John Ohlert's mother. Ohlert built a large building there in about 1870 to house a general store, a post office, and a dance hall, which attracted many people as a social center. The building was later turned into a hotel. The dock and floats, leading to the store and post office, are maintained by the community of Olga.

The large number of deer on Orcas Island accounted for names such as Doe Island, Doebay, Deer Point, Buck Bay, and, on the other side of the island, Deer Harbor and Fawn Island.

Grindstone Harbor is located on the south shore of Orcas Island. Once inside the anchorage is good, but watch for the rocks in the entrance.

BELOW RIGHT: Grindstone Harbor. In 1983 the Washington State ferry *Elwha* went aground on the reef guarding the entrance. Cautiously piloted small craft should not be afraid to enter, however.

Not intended for navigation.

BELOW LEFT: The reefs at the entrance to Grindstone Harbor worry many skippers, but good piloting will avoid them.

DAVE CALHOUN

About 2 miles up the east shore of East Sound is **Cascade Bay**, named by Richards, probably for a falls at an outlet from an upland lake. This is the site of the famous Rosario Resort, which is discussed in detail in chapter 16.

East Sound extends northward another 3 miles, with the island's principal town of **Eastsound** at its head. (While the long inlet is written as two words—*East Sound*—the town is a single word—*Eastsound.*) **Fishing Bay** and **Ship Bay**, at the head of East Sound, are separated by a peninsula. In Ship Bay, access to shore is by dinghy only. In Fishing Bay, a day-use dock has been built along the east shore, a short distance from the town. The dock is small, but visiting boats can anchor out and take their dinghies to the dock. The dock provides access to Eastsound's stores, restaurants, and many facilities of value to the boating public. Eastsound also has a fine historical museum, housed in original cabins built by island pioneers. These cabins were carefully taken apart and moved, piece by piece, to the museum site, where they were reconstructed to form one building. Included in the displays are the famous Ethan Allen collection of Indian relics, pioneer tools and artifacts, and other historical items. A fireproof vault protects the more valuable pieces. A visit to the museum is an interesting and rewarding experience.

The west side of East Sound is fairly steep, with nothing of particular interest except for **Dolphin Bay**, a small bight offering little protection. Near the southern end are **Twin Rocks**, with a shoal extending from the shore out to them.

Gulls & Buoys Gifts and Darvill's Books and Gifts are two of the good shopping spots in Eastsound.

DAVE CALHOUN

An interesting feature of East Sound is a peculiar wind pattern. Many a skipper, visiting Rosario for the first time, has looked out to see whitecaps on the water and decided that, if the wind is blowing that hard in East Sound, it must really be kicking up outside in Rosario Strait. This is not necessarily so. Several times I have left Rosario in a heavy chop only to go through one of the passes and find Rosario Strait flat.

Rounding **Diamond Point** and **Shag Rock** to enter **Harney Channel**, the bow can be poked into a cute little cove just east of **Foster Point**. The cove has a 5-fathom depth, but not much protection from the southeast. It is, however, one of those places the small boat skipper delights in exploring.

Another such spot, a favorite of mine, is **Grindstone Harbor**, a bit west of Foster Point. For a time in the 1860's, Grindstone Harbor was the domain of the wandering Paul K. Hubbs. Apparently, Hubbs had the only grindstone in the area, so friends and acquaintances got into the habit of bringing their knives and tools to be sharpened. The traffic became so heavy that Hubbs started a trading post. His little

A view of the village of Eastsound, located at the head of East Sound. While no marine services are available, charts can be purchased at Eastsound. Eastsound has several good dining places and other shopping.

store did very well, until he abandoned it after suffering a heart attack. This friendly little cove has been called Grindstone Harbor (or Bay) ever since.

There are two rocks mid-channel in Grindstone Harbor's entrance. The rocks are covered with kelp and sometimes there is a privately maintained marker. *With a bit of caution and a depth sounder, the skipper of a small boat should have no trouble entering Grindstone Harbor, and will find this a delightful place to drop the hook.* Large-scale chart 18434 will help the skipper feel more confident.

Following along the south shore of Orcas Island, about 1 mile west of Grindstone Harbor, a peninsula jutting into the channel has the appearance of an island. On occasion I have enjoyed the little bight behind it for a lunch stop or an afternoon siesta.

This is a private marina in Harney Channel.

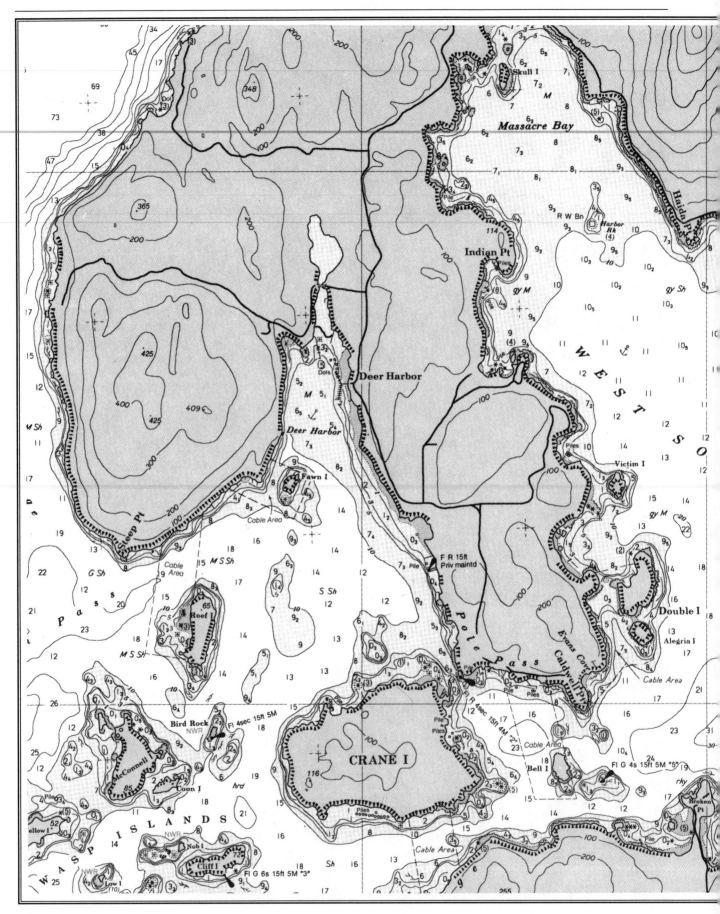

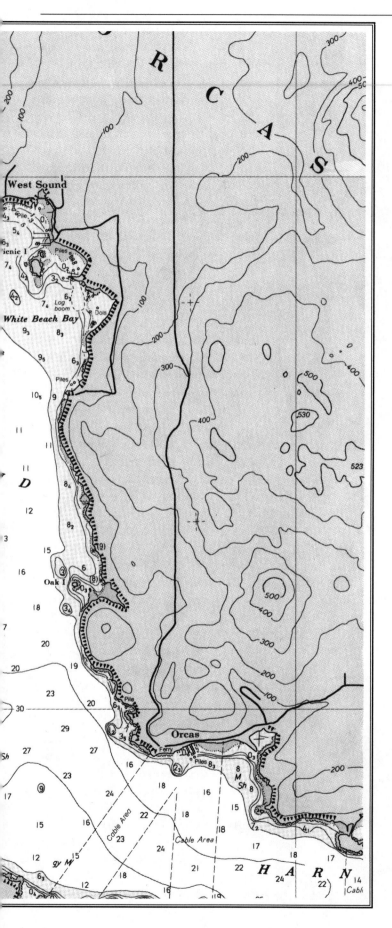

West Sound. The West Sound marina has haulouts, repairs, and a complete chandlery. The village of West Sound has a well-stocked store. Excellent anchorage can be had between Double Island and the peninsula.

Not intended for navigation.

The Washington State Ferry calls at the village of Orcas. Small boat moorage can be seen to the left of the ferry dock.

The fuel dock and short-term moorage at Orcas is exposed to the wash of passing boat traffic, so be sure your boat is well tied and well fendered.

A bit farther west is the village of **Orcas**. The ferry makes its Orcas Island stop there. The village has a grocery store, liquor store, fuel dock with fishing supplies, some gift shops, and a fast-food cafe with take-out or dine-in service. Orcas is also the location of the historic Orcas Hotel, with its overnight lodging, cocktail lounge, and elegant dining room, all in a quaint Victorian setting. The owners have put much time and effort into restoring this inn to its original form *circa* 1904. The Orcas Hotel is listed on the National Historical Register, and is a must-see attraction during a stop at Orcas Village. In mooring at the floats at Orcas, *it is well to leave someone aboard, or at least be sure the boat is well fendered, since washes from passing boats make a dangerous surge.*

Around the corner from the town of Orcas, **West Sound** extends north about 2½ miles, with **Massacre Bay** at its head. The several ominous-sounding names found here go back to Indian days, when fierce battles were fought between raiding tribes from the north and the local Lummi tribes. In addition to Massacre Bay, names such as **Indian Point**, **Haida Point**, **Skull Island**, and **Victim Island** all remind us of times when West Sound was not the peaceful haven it is today.

In behind Haida Point is a rather open bay with the community of **West Sound**, with store and deli, the Orcas Island Yacht Club, and the **West Sound Marina**. The marina offers complete boat and engine repair, with haulouts to 35 tons, and a chandlery. Just to the northwest of the marina, and to the left of the yacht club dock, is a county dock for daytime moorage while stocking up on groceries at the West Sound store or taking a short walk down the scenic country road. **Picnic Island** (sometimes called Sheep Island), just outside the marina, has some shoals and should be approached cautiously if the skipper does not have local knowledge. Although I have heard this entire bay to the east of Haida Point referred to as White Beach Bay, present charts show **White Beach Bay** only as the small bay to the southeast of Picnic Island. **Harbor Rock**, about

ABOVE: The West Sound Marina has ample dock space. Beware the shoals between the docks and Picnic Island.

LEFT: The West Sound Marina has fuel, haulouts and repairs, and a well-stocked chandlery in the building, right.

The fuel dock at Deer Harbor has good access, with transient moorage available.

midway between Indian Point and Haida Point, is marked with a beacon.

Haida Point is the southern extremity of Orcas Island's Turtleback Range, which rises to 1,500 feet and is the site of a mystery that remains unsolved to this day. Up near the top, made of rocks about the size of large grapefruit, is the outline of a ship's anchor. No one knows how it got there, but old-timers say it has been there as long as anyone can remember. The most generally accepted theory is that a sailing ship was wrecked somewhere along Orcas Island's west shore. Survivors are thought to have fashioned the anchor from rocks that were used as the ship's ballast. Whatever the anchor's source, it is an interesting addition to Orcas Island's lore. (*Editor's note:* Unfortunately, one must cross private property to get to the anchor. Local residents tell us the area is sufficiently overgrown that the general outline is obscured to a person standing at ground level. The anchor is there, but probably not worth the effort and permissions needed to find it.)

North of **Skull Island**, **Massacre Bay** is full of shoals, and rocks and reefs extend out a bit along the bay's scalloped west shore. Skull Island is owned by the Washington State Parks and Recreation Commission, and is held for future development. Within the wide bay below Indian Point is the private Four Winds Camp, with a good part of the campers' program being water-oriented.

Farther down the west shore is **Victim Island**. Victim Island, as is Skull Island, is owned by the Washington State Parks and Recreation Commission, and it too is being held for future development. A short distance south of Victim Island lies **Double Island**. Double Island is actually two islands, joined at low tide. *With care at higher stages of the tide, passage can be made behind Victim Island, but passage should not be attempted behind Double Island.*

There are a few good anchorages in West Sound. The best is behind Double Island, in the lee of its northwest shore. The cove is well protected and very pretty. Some protection can be found in the lower end of the bay below Indian Point, and in the nook north of Indian Point. Except for the state-owned Skull Island and Victim Island, all these shores are private and no landing should be made upon them. The shores of West Sound are sometimes referred to as The Gold Coast because of the many luxurious homes built there.

Rounding **Caldwell Point** heading for **Pole Pass**, *skippers of deeper draft vessels should watch out for a couple of shoals at low tide.* Check chart 18432. **Pole Pass** is formed between a tip of Orcas Island and a long point of **Crane Island**. A mere 75 feet wide, Pole Pass is the narrowest pass in the islands. Pole Pass was so named because the Indians strung nets on long poles across the pass to catch birds in a natural flyway.

Currents can run through Pole Pass at good velocity. Because of the narrow confines, skippers should use caution. *The approach to Pole Pass from the south has no dangers, but to the north a shoal extends out from Crane Island. There is also a shoal on the Orcas Island side, so a mid-channel course is called for, favoring the Orcas side a bit until well past these shoals.*

Deer Harbor is the third of Orcas Island's major waterways, indenting the westernmost leg of the island for about 1 mile. The **Deer Harbor Marina**, about midway up on the east shore, has excellent moorage, a fuel dock, and marine services. There are also a restaurant, a store, and overnight lodging in the

EDEN ARTS

Pole Pass, with Deer Harbor to the left, and West Sound to the Right. Follow piloting instructions to avoid rocks.

motel and cabins. A short hike up the road is Deer Harbor Inn and Restaurant with good food served country style. Lodging is available. For those who do not wish to walk, a phone call will bring a car for transport.

If you need repairs, Deer Harbor Boatworks has haulouts to 45 feet or 18 tons, and can handle most mechanical, woodworking, and fiberglass work.

At the entrance to Deer Harbor, *Fawn Island can be passed on either side, but skippers should be aware of the rock lying off the south end.*

North Pass, lying between the southwestern tip of Orcas Island and **Reef Island**, is 500 yards wide and has no hazards. North Pass brings us back to Steep Point, completing our circumnavigation of the island.

Orcas Island, with the largest number of resorts of any of the San Juans, frequently is called the Resort Island. You could say it all started with the Indians, when they came from the mainland to spend the summer in this paradise. As far back as the 1860's, pioneer records show people coming to the island to "summer" in tents on the beaches. Later there were hotels in Eastsound, but the first resort, as such, was started by the Nortons around 1910 at what is now the Deer Harbor Inn.

Each of the islands in the San Juan group has its own distinctive charm. Orcas Island is perhaps the richest in its multiplicity of both on-shore and off-shore delights. The island and its adjacent waterways form a near perfect cruising area for the skipper and crew.

C H A P T E R

9

THROUGH THE ROCK PILE

Yellow Island, between Orcas Island and
Shaw Island, now belongs to the Nature
Conservancy, and is open to visitors.

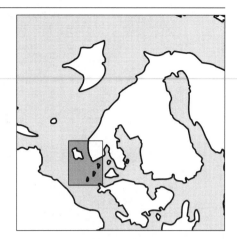

Bell Island
Crane Island
Reef Island
Bird Rock
McConnell Island
Coon Island
Yellow Island
Low Island
Cliff Island
Nob Island
Jones Island

In these days of fast boats, many skippers like to choose a specific destination or area, then speed to it at full throttle. For other skippers, cruising consists of short courses from resort to resort, or from favorite bays to other familiar spots. *All too many cruising families fail to take the time for leisurely exploration and careful investigation of some new area or point along the way.*

One of many intriguing possibilities for a sunny afternoon in the San Juans is an unhurried island-by-island cruise through the Rock Pile. The Rock Pile is a name given by some ferryboat skippers to that group of small islands, islets, and rocks lying between Orcas Island and Shaw Island, and charted as the Wasp Islands.

After reading or hearing early-day stories about the use of these islands as hiding places for smugglers, or for pirates preying on vessels using the narrow passes, one might guess the name Wasp was given to connote buzzing or stinging. Actually, Wilkes named the group for the U.S. sloop of war *Wasp*, which, under the command of Jacob Jones in the War of 1812, captured the British brig *Frolic*.

To enjoy this adventure, **be sure to have large-scale chart 18434, which shows in good detail the islands, the smaller islets, the rocks, and the reefs**. Then, paying close attention to the charted depths and the depth sounder, set out to do some real exploring in the Rock Pile. Take it slow—very slow. Enjoy the unique, varied beauty of this group. Be brave. Get in close. If you have a small boat so much the better, but I did it in a 36-footer with a 3½-draft and had no trouble. Make a game of the trip. Use a small-boy fantasy to find the best cove or nook to hide your smuggled silk or Canadian spirits from pursuing revenuers. Or, if piracy takes your fancy, pick the best place to hole up while waiting to make a sudden strike on an unsuspecting ship.

You might start at Pole Pass, as I did recently, and circle Crane Island clockwise, with a short side trip to investigate **Bell Island**. **Crane Island** has many different types of homes. It is fun to note how their owners have made use of a natural setting, with the hillsides, rocks, and trees combined to achieve their dreams of an island hideaway. Since there are plenty of rocks, shoals, and reefs around Crane Island, the skipper must not forget his piloting duties while enjoying the scenery. I think the key word is *slow*. Remember, too, that in the summer kelp marks most of the rock patches.

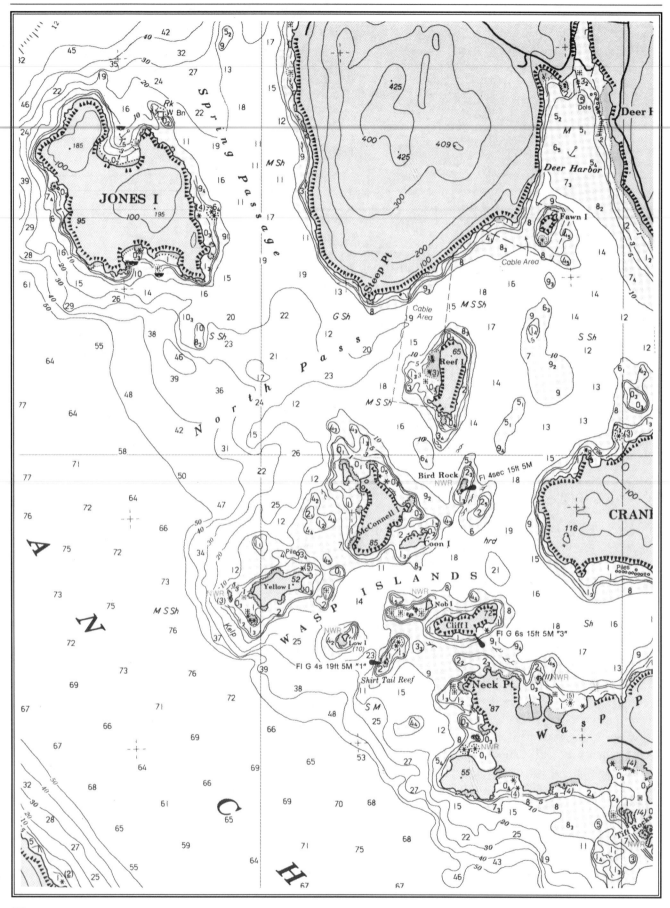

The cove at the north end of Jones Island is a state marine park, with picnic sites and water.

CHART OPPOSITE: The Wasp Islands. For the careful skipper the large-scale chart 18434 makes exploration less intimidating.

Not intended for navigation.

The north shore of Crane Island will bring you nearly back to Pole Pass, and a swing out is required to avoid the reef on the island's northeast corner. Next, you might take a run over to **Reef Island**. Wooded, ¼ of a mile long and 65 feet high, Reef Island is aptly named. *It is best to stay fairly well off the west side of Reef Island, and be aware of the shoal off the southern end.*

It might be interesting to circle **Bird Rock**, to observe the many cormorants inhabiting it. Because of their numbers, Bird Rock sometimes has been called Cormorant Rock. Probably you will agree that Bird Rock is best enjoyed from upwind.

This view of the cove at the north side of Jones Island shows the room and protection available.

RIGHT: The clear waters near Jones Island provide an inviting haven after a day of cruising.

BELOW: The coves on the south side of Jones Island offer some protection.

To the west is **McConnell Island**, with little **Coon Island** snuggling up to its southeast shore. **McConnell Island**, named for a pioneer family, is scenic, with several interesting little coves, and a point that almost becomes another island.

Today, McConnell Island is often visited by steam buffs or a whole fleet of steamboats of all sizes and shapes belonging to members of the Puget Sound Live Steamers. These visits are to inspect the miniature steam railroad system built by fellow member Tommy Thompson.

Islanders love to tell the story of the late, fun-loving Jack Tusler, who lived on **Coon Island** until his death in 1962. It seems that Jack Tusler loved to tickle his sense of humor by producing pantomime shows for the entertainment of ferry passengers. On a small flat rock a bit to the north of the ferries' course through Wasp Passage, Tusler would place an Indian in full regalia smoking a peace pipe, or a beautiful girl in mermaid costume combing her long, golden tresses. Other such diversions included a white-coated barber giving a man a haircut, or two couples at a card table playing bridge, or a surgeon performing an operation. Ferry passengers never knew what kind of "spectacular" the "Commodore of Coon Island" might devise for their amusement on the lone rock just off the main channel. The island is still privately owned and you should not go ashore.

To the southwest of McConnell Island is **Yellow Island**, something of a phenomenon in this area of lush growth. Yellow Island has trees, but it also has barren, almost desert-like areas growing prickly

A view of the light on the south side of Cliff Island, facing Wasp Passage.

DAVE CALHOUN

Pole Pass is narrow but well-traveled. Watch the chart for rocks and plot your course accordingly.

DAVE CALHOUN

Nob Island is shown here almost hiding behind the western tip of Cliff Island. Note the rocks stretching toward the left side of the photo. These are the kinds of conditions that make piloting in the Rock Pile interesting.

cactus plants. The island is owned by the Nature Conservancy and is open to the public. No picnics or camping are allowed, but in the spring the flowers are a sight to behold. The caretakers will familiarize you with the rules for enjoying Yellow Island. The best anchorage is in the southern cove, where you can dinghy ashore. You will find there an interesting home built several years ago entirely of materials beachcombed in the area. *Yellow Island requires the skipper to use caution as he picks his way among the rocks and reefs. Pay particular attention to the shoals extending a good 200 yards off the western tip.*

Low Island, small and about 10 feet high, is southeast of Yellow Island and has shoals on the west and south sides. To the east a bit is **Cliff Island**. A light on a point marks the channel of **Wasp Passage**. **Nob Island**, with a nob some 40 feet high, and its two tiny satellite isles are to the northwest. *Watch the charted rocks.*

Captain Richards is credited with naming most of the islands in this group. I wonder, however, if he is responsible for **Shirt Tail Reef**. With its light and echo board, this reef forms the southern limit of the Rock Pile.

If you have the urge and the courage to explore these island-studded waterways with their picturesque rocks and reefs, you will have fun. Look back. Let your fancy see smugglers dodging in and out of these isles to elude a customs man in his lumbering, low-powered launch. The smugglers knew these intricate waterways as a professional pilot knows his harbor approaches, and they were not often caught. There is romance here to intrigue the soul and challenge the imagination of the real seafaring man.

A mile or so to the northwest of the Wasp group, off the southwest corner of Orcas Island, is **Jones Island**, a state marine park. Jones Island was named by Wilkes for Jacob Jones, the captain of the *Wasp*. Nicely wooded, this 179-acre island has three hills reaching 110, 185, and 195 feet, with good trails for loosening up stiffened sea legs or letting the youngsters run off energy.

The bay on the north side of Jones Island offers good anchorage in 1 to 8 fathoms, with dock, float, and moorage buoys. It has a good gravel beach, and picnic facilities, tables, stoves, camp sites, and toilets. The small bays on the south side of Jones Island provide very little protection, but the beaches can be used by small boats. *Watch for a couple of charted rocks.*

A rock that bares at 2 feet lies about 150 yards off Jones Island's northeast point. The rock is marked, and surrounded by kelp. Fishing is usually good on the west side of the island and the beaches have clams. A shoal and a couple of rocks on the east side in Spring Passage are well marked by kelp.

Jones Island is a fine place to spend the night after an exploration of the Wasp Islands. Do not let the Rock Pile frighten you. Armed with the large-scale chart, a depth sounder or lead line, and good eyes, the adventuresome but careful skipper should have no trouble. Going aground, however, is not an unforgivable event in this kind of cruising. Remember, it is the skipper who never does anything who never makes a mistake. As the saying goes, "Try it, you'll like it!" A cruise through the San Juans' Rock Pile waterways will be both challenging and rewarding.

Bay on Jones Island

CHAPTER

10

SHAW ISLAND

This point on Shaw Island juts between Picnic
Cove and the entrance to Indian Cove.

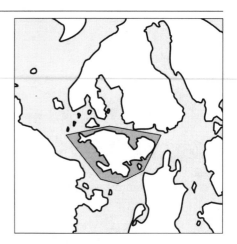

avorite bays, snug coves, a sandy beach; rugged, rocky shores; wooded uplands, friendly people, and a quiet, rustic mood—these are some of the qualities to be found in the San Juan Islands. Shaw Island has them all.

Shaw Island is roughly triangular in shape, and, because of its central location, often is called the hub of the islands. Shaw is one of the four islands served by ferry. The ferryboat slip is at the little village of Shaw on the northeast point of Blind Bay, located diagonally across Harney Channel from the ferry landing at Orcas.

Harney Channel was named by Richards for Brigadier General William S. Harney of the U.S. Army. Harney sent company D of the 9th Infantry, commanded by Captain George E. Pickett, to San Juan Island in July 1859 at the beginning of the boundary dispute. Shaw Island was named by Wilkes for Captain John D. Shaw, who served on the *Decatur*, a ship that played a prominent part in the war against Algiers in 1851.

While the perimeter of Shaw Island offers many attractions to yachtsmen, there is not much of interest ashore, not even a resort. The residents like it that way and do not seem interested in encouraging tourism, which is becoming the major industry on some of the other islands. Shaw Island almost had a resort back in the 1940's, when a Northwest yachtsman named Harold Salvesen planned to turn the old passenger ship *Admiral Rogers* into a shoreside resort in Blind Bay. The scheme fell through and Shaw Island was allowed to continue its quiet rural life, unbothered by the demands of city folks trying to escape their tensions.

A post office is at the Little Portion Store at the ferry landing, and a museum is about 2½ miles along the road. A small marina lies in the cove behind the ferry slip, where temporary moorage usually is available. The docks are exposed, so secure well, with ample fendering.

Although fishing, farming, cattle raising, and chickens occupy most of the residents today, Shaw Island has had other industries in the past. In the late 1800's limestone was quarried. Later, considerable cord wood was cut to supply the kilns at Roche Harbor. There were a fish cannery and a fruit cannery on Blind Bay, as well as two boat works that turned out both large and small pleasure and commercial vessels.

Neck Point
Parks Bay
Hicks Bay
Hoffman Cove
Indian Cove
Picnic Cove
Blind Bay
Broken Point

FOLLOWING PAGE: Shaw Island. Several appealing coves call the cruiser. Two of the most popular are Parks Bay, on the southwest corner, and Blind Bay on the north side.

Not intended for navigation.

93

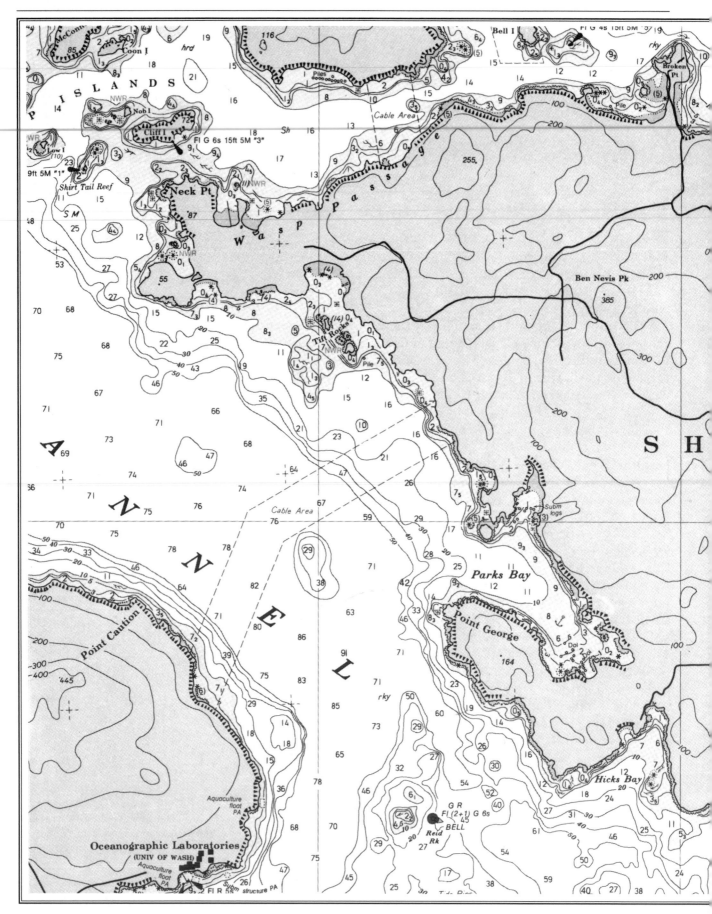

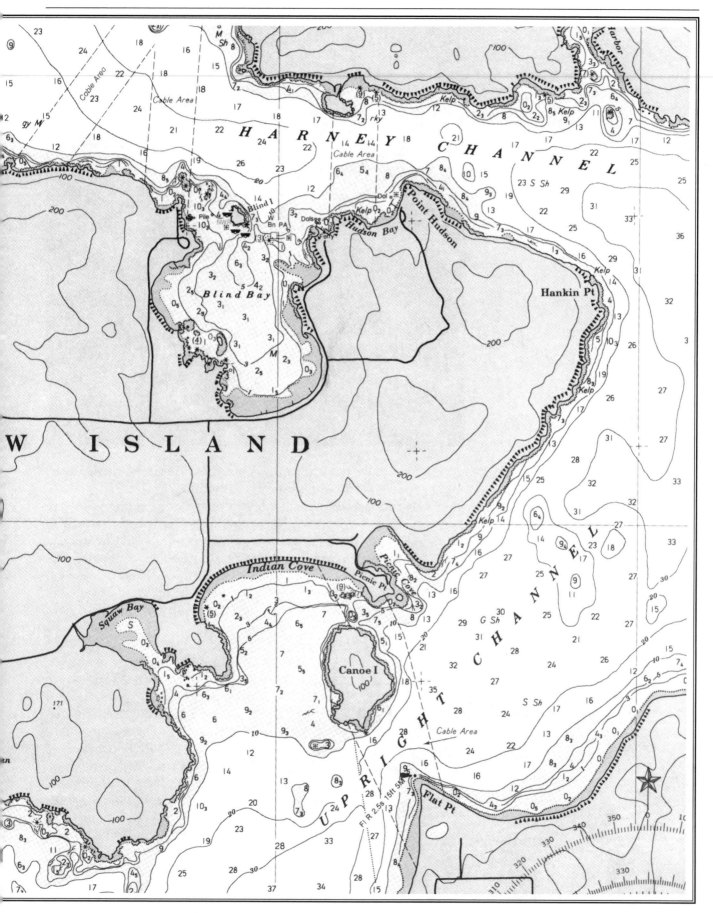

W ISLAND

BLIND BAY

Blind I

Blind Bay

HARNEY CHANNEL

Kelp

Point Hudson

Hudson Bay

Hankin Pt

Kelp

Kelp

Kelp

Squaw Bay

Indian Cove

Picnic Pt

Picnic Cove

Kelp

Canoe I

UPRIGHT CHANNEL

Cable Area

G Sh

S Sh

Fl R 2.5s 15ft 5M

Flat Pt

EDEN ARTS

Parks Bay is a popular anchorage on Shaw Island. This is the view looking southeast.

Reef netters try their luck in the waters off Shaw Island. The net is stretched between the two boats.

At one time there was a post office on the west side of Shaw Island and, later, a post office at the head of Blind Bay.

Shaw Island's residents, both year-round and summer only, are a peaceful lot today, but such has not always been the case. In the days of smuggling, the difference between the price of wool in Canada and in the United States made it profitable to slip wool past the customs man. A leader in this endeavor was Shaw islander Alfred Burke, who did a flourishing business at shearing time, as he furtively crossed and recrossed the water to buy or trade for wool in the Canadian Gulf Islands. He sold the wool to sheep ranchers in the San Juans, who mixed it with their own fleeces and sold it for high profits.

Through a clever ruse, inspectors finally identified some Canadian wool in a warehouse on Orcas Island. Burke was charged with smuggling, but was acquitted because no one testified to seeing him cross the border with the wool.

There was further excitement on Shaw Island when a farmer named Hugh Parks so far outshone his neighbors in industry and in developing his place that he made the neighbors jealous. After a few years their taunts were too much for

Parks. He ended his own life, after first shooting three of his tormentors and then holding off the sheriff and posse until they burned his house down.

In 1874, some years after the end of the bloodless Pig War and the settlement of the boundary dispute, Shaw Island was the site of two of seven government reservations chosen by a team of army engineers for possible military fortifications. For a time, the British in Victoria were reported to be extremely worried over this development. However, after General William Tecumseh Sherman visited the sites, it was learned that they had been chosen as protectorate bases to guard Griffin Bay should it ever be needed as a refuge for American ships. These fortifications were never built.

Top: Canoe Island protects the entrance to Indian Cove on Shaw Island's Upright Channel side. This view is from the southeast.

Bottom: This is the pass behind Canoe Island, as seen from water level.

Two decades ago Bruce Calhoun found this junk anchored peacefully in Blind Bay. Unusual boats still are commonplace in the San Juans.

Blind Island and a number of rocks visible in this photo guard the entrance to Blind Bay. By following piloting advice, safe entry can be made with ease.

EDEN ARTS

In 1971 Shaw Island became the hub of an annual sailboat race. Known as the Shaw Island Sailboat Classic, each year the race around the island attracts as many as 100 boats in four classes. While the majority of the entries are from the islands, some come from Portland, Bellingham, Anacortes, and many other ports south.

My most recent inspection of Shaw Island's shores started at **Neck Point**. We found, as we had on many previous visits, that a bit of beachcombing by boat can be rewarding. With large-scale chart 18434 as an everpresent guide, it is fun to skirt the shore, poking into the coastline with its bays and coves, ducking in behind little isles, rocks, and reefs.

After rounding the westernmost point of Shaw Island just below Neck Point, we received the usual greeting from the shore — opening doors and friendly waves. It would seem that, while residents have an unlimited view of San Juan Channel with its traffic of large and small vessels, they feel a special kinship for those coming in close enough for a neighborly greeting. If you use a bit of caution the little isles offshore can safely be passed inside on the higher stages of the tide. The scenic beauty offers some good photographic possibilities.

The principal feature on Shaw Island's west side is **Parks Bay**, named for that much harassed farmer of early days. Snuggled in behind **Point George** and with wooded shores, Parks Bay is a comfortable as well as beautiful anchorage, a favorite of yachtsmen over the years. *The delightful little cove off the north end of Parks Bay has pilings and submerged logs, so it should be entered, if at all, with due caution.* Parks Bay has a shoal extending out from its head but is otherwise clear, with 5 to 11 fathoms and a soft bottom. Land around the bay is privately owned and posted, so there is no going ashore.

Around Point George on Shaw Island's south side are **Hicks Bay** and little **Hoffman Cove**. Both are exposed to southerly winds but otherwise offer some protection. Rocks and reefs along the shore of Hicks Bay and a larger reef off the east shore near the outside are all well marked with kelp. Hoffman Cove has a nice beach at its head.

On the southeastern side of Shaw Island are three interesting and attractive indentations. **Squaw Bay** and **Indian Cove** are separated by a wide peninsula. While nearly landlocked, **Squaw Bay** is too shallow to be of much use. There are shoals on both sides of the entrance, as well as along all the shores. Depths of only 4½ feet in mid-channel shoal to 1½ feet near the middle at zero tide. *Unless you are in a small, shallow-draft boat or use the dinghy, it is better not to go into Squaw Bay except at higher tide.*

Indian Cove, or **South Beach** as local residents call it, has what is probably the finest sandy beach in the entire archipelago. Since part of Indian Cove is a county park, it is available to the skippers of small boats. This property was one of the original military reservations of the 1870's, and was purchased from the government by island residents for use as a park. The park begins at about the halfway point along the beach at the boat landing ramp. It has picnic tables, eight campsites, toilets, and fresh water. The beach shoals out for some 200 yards before it reaches a depth of 6 feet, so larger boats should not approach too close.

This is the ferry landing at Shaw Island. Some dock space is available to the left.

Canoe Island, wooded and pretty, forms an eastern buffer for Indian Cove. The site of French Camp, Canoe Island is privately owned and in the summertime you may see people hiking, sailing, canoeing, or rowing near its shores. Kids come to this lovely island to learn the language and culture of the French. Canoe Island has a shoal extending from its southeastern point. *Safe passage can be made to the north of the island, but the course should favor the Canoe Island side of the channel to avoid a ¾-fathom patch in mid-channel.*

Tucked in behind another peninsula to the north is charming little **Picnic Cove**. Although the inner shores shoal out a bit, there are 6 to 10 feet of depth in the middle at low tide to form a delightful little gunkhole that should not be passed by. The beach, of course, is private, but I have found the cove an enjoyable place to wet the anchor for a lunch stop.

Continuing northeast in **Upright Channel**, we round **Hankin Point** to enter **Harney Channel**. Three-quarters of a mile northwest, **Point Hudson** forms **Hudson Bay**. Hudson Bay is quite open and the cable from Orcas Island crosses there, so it is not recommended as a harbor.

To the west a bit is **Blind Bay**, with **Blind Island** in the entrance. Blind Island is a Washington State marine park, and has four mooring buoys, a pit toilet, and picnic tables with fire pits, but no drinking water or garbage service. Blind Bay is frightening to many skippers, because of shoals, rocks, and old pilings that make the entrance a bit demanding. Actually, Blind Bay is a nice, protected harbor, but certain cautions should be observed. *In entering Blind Bay, Blind Island can be passed on its* west *side after careful study of chart 18434 to avoid several rocks to the northwest, as well as a piling, a shoal and another rock.*

The best entrance, however, is to the *east* of Blind Island. A shoal extends southward for about 75 yards. *If you stay off just far enough to avoid the shoal, it is easy to miss the rock and reef which extend nearly to mid-channel from the northeast point of the bay.* Inside there is good depth of 6 feet and more if you stay 150 yards off the shallow shores. In the southwest part of Blind Bay is a scenic little rock island, surrounded by reefs. It is probably not wise to go behind the island, at least at low tide. I found a good-sized Chinese junk anchored in Blind Bay on my last visit. So do not bypass this pleasant anchorage. Use the chart and a little caution and you will like it.

100

DAVE CALHOUN

A water level view of the dock adjacent to Shaw Island's ferry landing.

The rest of Shaw Island's north coast has several pleasant little coves and bights that are fun to explore, but unfortunately do not offer much in the way of good anchorage. **Broken Point** is a long peninsula stretching up toward West Sound to form Shaw Island's northernmost point, at the entrance to Wasp Passage. Some protection for a lunch stop can be found on either side, depending on wind direction. Check the chart carefully on the west side for the shoals, reefs, and rocks, which usually are well marked by kelp. There is some good scenic beachcombing to be enjoyed along the Shaw Island side of Wasp Passage up to Neck Point, but, again, take it very slow. Watch the chart and depth sounder and you will have a safe passage.

Add Shaw Island to the gems in the San Juan crown that you must explore. Shaw Island is different, as is each of the islands, and it offers the cruising family not only its pleasant surrounding waters for exploration but also interesting things to see during shore leave.

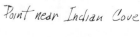

Point near Indian Cove

11

THE PIG WAR STORY

Before restoration, the barracks that housed British troops on San
Juan Island during the Pig War almost crumbled into history.

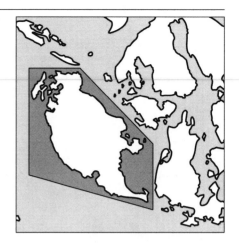

In the summer of 1859 San Juan Island was an international tinderbox. While sheep grazed peacefully on the green slopes of Bellevue Farm, military forces of Great Britain and the United States stood face-to-face in a confrontation that could at any moment erupt in violence and possibly plunge the two nations into war. The cause of the crisis: *the shooting of a pig.*

The Pig War, as the confrontation on San Juan Island came to be called, is so inextricably a part of the history and background of the islands that we cannot ignore it. Most Northwest yachtsmen have heard of the bloodless battle. Some know the whole story. Others have only a cursory knowledge of the facts.

Since I believe that maximum enjoyment of cruising in the San Juans calls for at least a casual acquaintance with the history of the area, the Pig War must be given attention. For those wishing a detailed account, I heartily recommend David Richardson's interesting and well-researched book, *Pig War Islands*, mentioned in an earlier chapter. For the more condensed version given here I am indebted to the National Park Service of the U.S. Department of the Interior, which has made the grounds where this war was "fought" a national historical park.

The so-called Pig War had its beginnings in the Anglo-American dispute over possession of the Oregon Country. The Oregon Country was a vast expanse of land that included the present states of Washington, Oregon, and Idaho, part of Montana and Wyoming, and the province of British Columbia. At the beginning of the 19th century this land was claimed by four nations: Spain, Russia, England, and the United States. Spain gave up her claim in 1819, when the Adams-Onis Treaty established the 42nd parallel as the northern boundary of California. Russia withdrew in 1824-25, when the Czar signed treaties with both England and the United States ceding all claims south of latitude 54°40'. Between 1825 and 1846 American pioneers battled British fur traders for control of that region between the 42nd parallel and latitude 54°40'.

An Anglo-American agreement of 1818 provided for joint occupation of the Oregon Country. By 1845, however, this agreement had become intolerable to the Americans, who considered it an afront to Manifest Destiny. Motivated by intense pride generated during the

Jacksonian era, American pioneers maintained the firm belief that continental expansion was the nation's destiny, and that whoever stood in the way of that destiny should be swept aside. They believed it to be right, just, and necessary that the social and political benefits of American culture be spread from ocean to ocean, from pole to pole. "Who shall undertake to define the limits of the expansibility of the population of the United States?" asked Caleb Cushing in his Report on the Territory of Oregon in 1839.

Cushing continued, "Does it [the American frontier] not flow westward with the never-easing advance of a rising tide of the sea? Along a line of more than a thousand miles from the lakes to the Gulf of Mexico, perpetually moves forward the western frontier…. Occasionally, an obstacle presents itself in some unproductive region of the country; or some Indian tribe; the column is checked; its wings incline toward each other; it breaks; but it speedily reunites again beyond the obstacle, and resumes its forward program, ever facing and approaching nearer and nearer to the remotest regions of the west…. This movement goes on with predestined certainty, and the unerring precision of the great works of eternal Providence, rather than as an act of feeble man. Another generation may see the

British Marines stand formation outside their Barracks on San Juan Island in 1867 during the Pig War.

settlement of our people diffused over the Pacific slopes of the Rocky Mountains."

To many Americans, it was unacceptable that the great land west of the Rocky Mountains should remain under foreign influence. By mid-century the spirit of Manifest Destiny had carried the American frontier west to the Pacific and north to far western Canada.

The British were determined to resist the tide of American migration that was sweeping across the Rockies and into the Oregon Country. The British argued that the Americans had no right to settle there, that the Americans were, in fact, trespassing on land guaranteed to England by treaties with Spain and Russia. These treaties, it was pointed out, entitled England to all the land west of the Rocky Mountains, from the northern boundary of California and Nevada to the southern tip of the Alaska Panhandle. Moreover, the British claimed ownership on the basis of early explorations by James Cook, George Vancouver, and Alexander Mackenzie, and on the use of the Oregon Country by the long-established fur-trading posts and commercial establishments of the Hudson's Bay Company, the foremost of which was Fort Vancouver on the Columbia River. The weakness of the legally valid British claim, however, lay in Britain's failure to homestead the region and give it identity.

Although both nations blustered and threatened over possession of the Oregon Country, neither sought to gain control of the whole region. The United States was willing to settle for an extension of the 49th parallel to the Pacific. Great Britain, on the other hand, would agree to the Columbia River as the southern boundary of western Canada, because she considered ownership of the river vital for command of the interior fur trade. Thus, the region actually in dispute was the triangle of land between the 49th parallel and the Columbia River. By 1845, with 5,000 Americans living in the Willamette Valley as compared to 750 Britons gathered mostly around Fort Vancouver and Puget Sound, a local clash certainly was possible. Indeed, there were some among the Americans who threatened to cross the Columbia and drive out the Hudson's Bay Company and set fire to its establishments, thus ending its influence.

After two years of belligerent talk in the legislative halls of Great Britain and the United States and in the public press of both countries, wiser counsels prevailed and the Oregon question was resolved peacefully. The Oregon Treaty of June 1846 gave the United States undisputed possession of the Pacific Northwest south of the 49th parallel, extending the boundary " ... to the middle of the channel which separates the continent from Vancouver's Island; and thence southerly from the middle of the said channel, and the Fuca's strait to the Pacific Ocean." But while the treaty settled the larger boundary question, it created a new problem. Its wording left unclear who owned the choicest of the San Juan Islands. The dispute that had brought the threat of war over the Oregon Territory was to be reenacted in miniature over the ownership of these islands.

The difficulty arose over the interpretation of that portion of the boundary described as the "middle of the channel" separating Vancouver Island from the mainland. The men who negotiated the

Oregon Treaty, like so many 19th century statesmen who drew boundary lines on crude maps, seem to have had little accurate geographic knowledge of the area whose fate they were deciding. There were, as you can see, actually two channels: Haro Strait, nearer Vancouver Island, and Rosario Strait, nearer the mainland. The San Juan Islands lay between the two. The British realized that possession of the islands, particularly San Juan Island, would give them complete control of the nearby harbors of Victoria and Esquimalt, as well as control of the approach to the Fraser River. Great Britain therefore insisted that the boundary was meant to run through Rosario Strait. The Americans, reinforced by the unequivocal doctrine of Manifest Destiny, proclaimed that the boundary lay through Haro Strait. Thus both sides considered the San Juan Islands theirs for settlement.

As early as 1845 the Hudson's Bay Company had posted a notice of possession on San Juan Island. In 1850 the company established a salmon-curing station there, and, three years later, a sheep ranch called Bellevue Farm. About the same time, the territorial legislature of Oregon (an area which then included the present state of Washington) declared the San Juan Islands to be within its territorial limits. In January 1853, the territorial legislature incorporated the San Juans into Island County. When Washington Territory was created in March 1853, the San Juans were attached to Whatcom County, Washington Territory's northernmost county. A U.S. customs collector for the District of Puget Sound was assigned to San Juan Island.

Meanwhile, the Hudson's Bay sheep farm was successful and growing, and neither the farm nor the British government recognized the legislative actions taken to remove San Juan Island from its

This is British Camp's blockhouse on the shores of Garrison Bay, before it was restored.

jurisdiction. When the U.S. customs officer attempted to levy duties on the company's imports, the company refused to pay, whereupon the sheriff of Whatcom County assessed the farm's property, seized some sheep, and sold them at auction. The Hudson's Bay Company hotly protested the seizure and demanded several thousand dollars in damages. To smooth over an ugly situation, U.S. Secretary of War William L. Marcy proposed that an American and British commission be set up to study and try to resolve the boundary problem. The commission met in 1857 but settled nothing.

By 1859 about 25 Americans were living on San Juan Island. They were settled on redemption claims, recognized as valid by the U.S. government, but considered illegal by the British. Compounding the problem was the fact that some of the Americans were settled on land earlier claimed by the Hudson's Bay Company. Neither side recognized the authority of the other. Tempers were short and little was needed to produce a crisis.

On June 15, 1859, the needed incident occurred. An American settler named Lyman Cutler saw a pig belonging to Charles Griffin, the manager of the Hudson's Bay sheep farm, destroying his small potato patch. In a moment of anger, Cutler shot and killed the pig. Cutler agreed to pay for the animal, but an angry Griffin demanded $100 in damages. When Cutler, who thought the pig worth no more than $10, refused to pay, Griffin called in Alexander Dallas, the president of the Council of the Hudson's Bay Company in North America. Cutler considered Dallas's manner and language both insulting and abusive. When Dallas threatened to take Cutler to Victoria for trial, Cutler reminded Dallas that, as an American citizen living on American soil, he was not subject to British jurisdiction. Dallas withdrew, taking no action, but making it plain that the affair was not finished. The Pig War had begun.

The rebuilt blockhouse on Garrison Bay at British Camp makes for interesting exploration.

The commissary building at British Camp on San Juan Island before the building was restored.

The commissary building at British Camp as it appears today, restored.

Fearing reprisal, the American settlers on San Juan Island petitioned Brigadier General William S. Harney, a Mexican War veteran commanding the Department of Oregon, to protect them in their "present exposed and defenseless position" against the British. As further justification for their request for military protection, the settlers cited the fierce and warlike Haida Indians of the north, who frequently came down from the Strait of Georgia and the fjords of British Columbia and Russian Alaska to raid the area around Puget Sound.

General Harney, who held strong anti-British attitudes and who looked upon San Juan Island as a fit location for a U.S. naval station, saw in the settlers' petition an excellent opportunity to force the sovereignty issue. Reacting swiftly, he ordered Captain George E. Pickett (later to gain fame at Gettysburg but in 1859 commanding Company D, 9th Infantry) to occupy San Juan Island with his troops.

DAVE CALHOUN

Pickett, according to his orders, was first to protect the inhabitants of the island from incursions by the northern Indians and secondly "to afford adequate protection to American citizens" from British authorities.

Pickett's unit of 66 men landed on July 27, 1859, and occupied a high ridge overlooking Eagle Cove, just north of Bellevue Farm. This position commanded Griffin Bay (then called San Juan Harbor) on the north, and the water approaches from the south. After mounting one six-pounder cannon and two howitzers to defend his men against British interference, Pickett announced that San Juan Island was under American jurisdiction and its inhabitants subject only to American laws.

James Douglas, the governor of the new Crown colony of British Columbia, was outraged at the presence of American soldiers on San Juan Island, and dispatched three British warships to dislodge Pickett. The troops were to avoid an armed clash if possible. Pickett, though overwhelmingly outnumbered, refused to withdraw and, according to General Harney, "nobly replied that whether they [the British] landed fifty or five thousand men, his conduct would not be affected by it; he would open his fire…." Throughout the remaining days of July and well into August, the British force in Griffin Bay continued to grow in strength. The ships' officers wisely refused to take any action against the Americans until Rear Admiral Robert L. Baynes, commander of the British naval forces

Another view of the British barracks at British Camp on Garrison Bay, before the building was restored.

The restored barracks building at British Camp are part of a self-guided tour of the park.

DAVE CALHOUN

As part of the British Camp park development, archaeological digs were conducted to search for artifacts and historical information.

This gravestone at British Camp is a reminder of the British military presence, and the fact that even without hostilities, some troops never went home.

in the Pacific, arrived with instructions. Baynes was appalled at the situation and advised Douglas that he would "not involve two great nations in a war over a squabble about a pig."

Pickett, in the meantime, had been reinforced on August 10 by 64 men under Lieutenant Colonel Silas Casy, but his meager force was still no match for the growing concentration of British vessels and men. Using carrier pigeons, Pickett apprised General Harney of the vulnerability of his position. General Harney ordered reinforcements. By August 31, some 461 Americans, protected by 14 cannons and an earthwork, were facing five British warships mounting 167 guns and carrying a troop strength of 2,140 men, including Royal Marines, artillerymen, sappers, and miners. The initiative lay in the hands of the British, but Admiral Baynes, over Douglas's angry protests, would not commit his force unless compelled to do so.

By this time word of the crisis had reached Washington, where officials were shocked to learn that the simple action of an irate farmer had grown into an explosive international incident. Greatly alarmed, the acting Secretary of War cautioned Harney that, while he was not to allow the national honor to be tarnished by the British, "it would be a shocking event if the two nations should be precipitated into a war." Meanwhile, Lieutenant General Windfield Scott, the commanding general of the U.S. Army, was sent to investigate the affair. Scott arrived at Fort Vancouver on October 20 and reported, "I found both Brigadier General Harney and Captain Pickett proud of their conquest of the island and quite jealous of interference." Harney was officially rebuked and afterwards recalled, for allowing the situation to get out of hand and teeter on the brink of war.

The British ships were drawn off and negotiations with the Governor of British Columbia were opened at Fort Townsend, Washington. Both sides agreed to Scott's suggestion that a token force from each nation occupy San Juan until a final settlement could be reached. Pickett's soldiers were withdrawn and replaced by others under a different officer. On March 21, 1860, Royal Marines landed on the island's northwest coast and established at Garrison Bay what is now known as British Camp.

San Juan Island remained under joint military occupation for the next 12 years. Negotiations were discontinued during the Civil War years, and, while the American force was reduced to a handful of men, the British did not take advantage of the Americans' situation. Local tradition says that the settlers and the soldiers were at least relatively friendly, with all parties celebrating major holidays together. A road was built connecting the military camps and the island gradually adjusted to peaceful occupation by the two countries.

In 1871, when Great Britain and the United States signed the Treaty of Washington, the San Juan question was referred to Kaiser Wilhelm I of Germany for settlement. On October 21, 1872, the emperor ruled for the United States, establishing the boundary line through Haro Strait. Thus the San Juans became an American possession and the final boundary between Canada and the United States was set. On November 25, 1872, the Royal Marines withdrew from British Camp. By July 1874, the last of the U.S. troops left American Camp. Peace finally had come to the 49th parallel, and San Juan Island long would be remembered for a military confrontation in which the only casualty was a pig.

American Camp is on the barren and windswept southeast tip of San Juan Island, about five miles from Friday Harbor. While no buildings survive, their original locations are known. The National Park Service plans to define and restore the grounds and earthworks. The remains of Pickett's redoubt, the principal American defense work, are well preserved. The redoubt originally contained gun platforms and heavy cannon designed to cover Griffin Bay and the Juan de Fuca Strait. The American Camp site is near the present Cattle Point Road and Pickett's redoubt. Surviving foundations and blackened posts are believed to be the sites of a hospital and a row of officers' quarters.

The old San Juan Town, the first settlement in the Griffin Bay area, was just east of a small tidal pool on the north side of American Camp. The town, legend has it, was a notorious and lively community. It was destroyed by fire in 1890 and only a few cellar depressions remain.

British Camp lies in the tree-sheltered cove known as Garrison Bay, about eight miles from Friday Harbor. Three structures built during the British occupation still stand: the blockhouse, a two-story log structure on the eastern shore of the bay; the commissary, a one-story gable structure north of the blockhouse; and the barracks directly across from the commissary. On a rise next to the Crook House are the remains of a blacksmith shop that served the camp.

DAVE CALHOUN

This monument to the settling of the Pig War boundary dispute can be found at American Camp on San Juan Island.

Officers' quarters were on a low ridge overlooking the barracks. Only the foundations of three houses remain; they are moss-covered and nestled under some large trees. The British cemetery, just beyond the officers' quarters and up Mt. Young, is a small, fenced plot, where seven Royal Marines who died during the occupation are buried. A marker was placed at the site by the Royal Canadian Navy in 1964.

San Juan Island National Historical Park, recently renamed British Camp, is administered by the National Park Service and is open daily from sunrise to sunset. Visitor facilities include restrooms, and in the summer there are rangers on duty and an information center with slide shows. You may anchor in Garrison Bay and dinghy into the park. There is a dinghy dock to tie to while you enjoy the rich history of the area.

These formal gardens at British Camp are on the shores of Garrison Bay.

Camping, picnicking, building fires, and hunting are forbidden. Firearms are not permitted in the park. Pets are permitted only when under physical control. Natural features and historical buildings or ruins are to be left undisturbed.

When I visited British Camp, I had mixed emotions about the fine restoration that had been done to the buildings and the general cleanup of the grounds. It must be acknowledged that, to preserve these historical buildings and keep them from collapsing, such restoration was necessary. Somehow, though, the nostalgia felt during previous visits was lacking.

American Camp is on a desolate,
wind-swept hill south of British Camp.

It was interesting to see the several spots where archeological digging was in progress, presumably for artifacts both from the occupation days and from earlier Indian life.

San Juan Islanders are keenly aware of these events of more than a century ago, and the end of the Pig War was memorialized in a centennial celebration during the summer of 1972. The Canadian vessel HMCS *Porte de la Reine* visited Friday Harbor to join the celebration. A softball game was played between its crew and local residents, and the crew hosted a barbecue on board the ship. On Memorial Day, members of the American and Canadian legions joined with military units of both countries at the British Camp cemetery to raise a Union Jack in tribute to the British Royal Marines.

Thus, memories of the Pig War continue to be woven into the ethereal fabric that is such an integral part of the magic of the islands. Cruising families should put San Juan Island on the itinerary's must list. Thanks to Charles Griffin's pig, the remnants of a colorful page of history await their exploration and enjoyment during a visit to this section of the San Juans.

CHAPTER

12

SAN JUAN ISLAND

The point behind Turn Island is typical of the
scenic delights of the San Juan Islands.

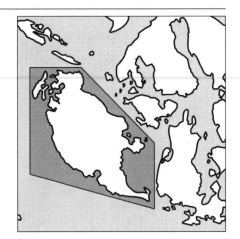

P erhaps the phrase Paradise Islets, frequently applied to the San Juan Islands, is more than fancy rhetoric. At least it was more than fancy rhetoric to the Indians who lived on the islands. An ancient legend of the Lummi tribe tells how their "First Man" descended from the sky hundreds of years ago to father the tribe. The First Man was supposed to have taken up residence in an aboriginal Garden of Eden located on the northeast corner of San Juan Island.

If the Lummis, who are known to have lived on San Juan Island, later on Orcas Island, and finally on the mainland, considered these islands to be a paradise, there is ample reason for present-day residents and cruising yachtsmen to take a similar view. Many elements combine to create the special charm of the islands. The typical

Cattle Pass
San Juan Channel
Salmon Bank
Fish Creek
Griffin Bay
Dinner Island
Turn Island
Friday Harbor
Rocky Bay
Barren Island
Posey Island
Roche Harbor
Mosquito Pass
Westcott Bay
Garrison Bay
Mitchell Bay
Smuggler's Cove

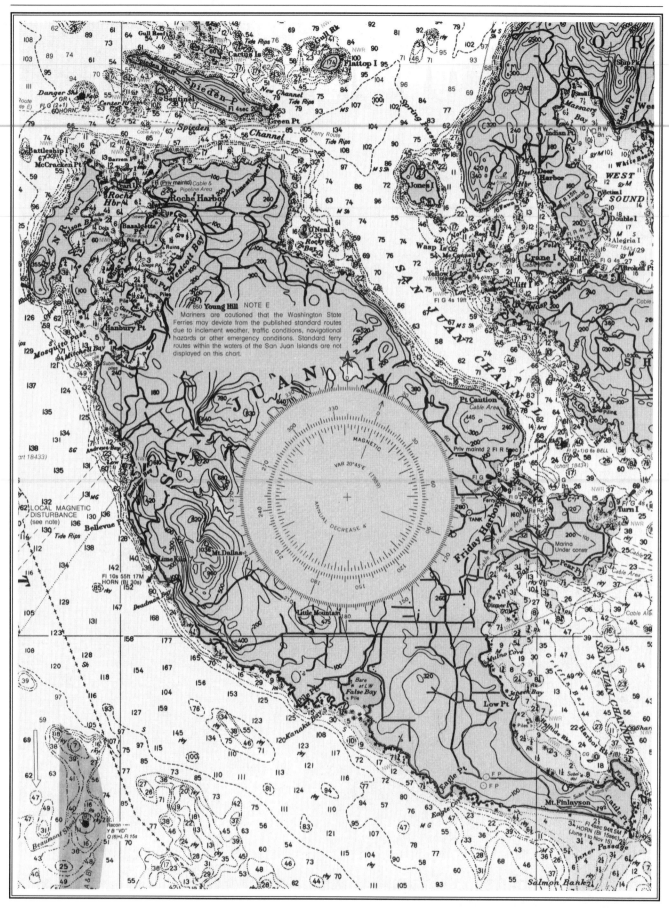

NOTE E

Mariners are cautioned that the Washington State Ferries may deviate from the published standard routes due to inclement weather, traffic conditions, navigational hazards or other emergency conditions. Standard ferry routes within the waters of the San Juan Islands are not displayed on this chart.

LOCAL MAGNETIC DISTURBANCE (see note)

MAGNETIC

VAR 20°45'E (1989)

ANNUAL DECREASE 4'

skipper, family, and guests do not try to analyze that charm—they just enjoy San Juan Island and see as much as possible.

One of these ingredients, certainly, is the peaceful, quiet, and relaxed life lived in the San Juans. The islands have not always enjoyed this peace, however. History records violence, lawlessness, bloodshed, and even murder on several of the islands, and San Juan Island has led in this respect.

Although the boundary dispute was not to come to a head with the pig episode until 1859, the uncertainty of ownership of the islands kept things in a turmoil for some years before. As early as 1845 the Hudson's Bay Company claimed possession of San Juan Island and erected a marker near Cattle Point. In 1850 the company established a fishing center at Eagle Cove on San Juan Island's southwest shore, and in 1852 it sent Charles Griffin over to the island with 1,300 sheep to start what became known as Bellevue Farm.

In the same year, 1852, the Oregon Territorial Legislature included the islands as part of Island County, and they continued so until 1855, when the new Washington Territorial Legislature made them a part of Whatcom County. Efforts of American officials to collect taxes—and of both countries to impose customs duties while the diplomats argued—resulted in many incidents, including some armed threats. No shots were actually fired, however.

During the 12 years of joint occupation, San Juan Island saw more settlers arrive, many of them disappointed gold seekers from the Fraser River gold rush. The first town, called San Juan Town and later known as Old Town, was started on Griffin Bay. With no sovereignty, no laws, no taxes, and the rough pioneer character of most of the settlers, misdeeds and crimes of all kind were rampant. Tempers flared easily. The military tried, not always successfully, to control these disorders. These 12 years were a period of anything but peace and tranquility on beautiful San Juan Island.

Conditions became more orderly after the boundary was established in 1872, although whiskey still flowed and there was still some lawlessness. Dan W. Oakes, Charles McKay, Stephen Boyce, and Edward D. Warbass were among the early settlers who played important parts in island development. Schools, churches, stores, and the town of Friday Harbor were established. Other small communities were started at Argyle and Madden's Corners. Both San Juan Town and Argyle were later destroyed by fire.

Friday Harbor continued to grow. When San Juan County was created, Friday Harbor became the county seat. There are two stories about the source of Friday Harbor's name. According to one story, a Kanaka sheepherder used to graze his flocks on the grassy slopes of the bay. The sheepherder was known as Joe Friday and this story says that early boatmen called the bay Friday's Harbor.

Visitors to Friday Harbor should not miss a trip to the Whale Museum. The exhibit within is far more spectacular than the modest entry suggests.

OPPOSITE: San Juan Island. Friday Harbor is the San Juan Islands' commercial center, with showers, shopping, and dining available. Roche Harbor, at the northeast corner, is a popular destination. Garrison Bay has good, protected anchorage.

Not intended for navigation

Turn Island

San Juan Island and surrounding islands,
as viewed from the northwest.

1. Speiden Island
2. Sentinal Island
3. San Juan Island
4. Henry Island

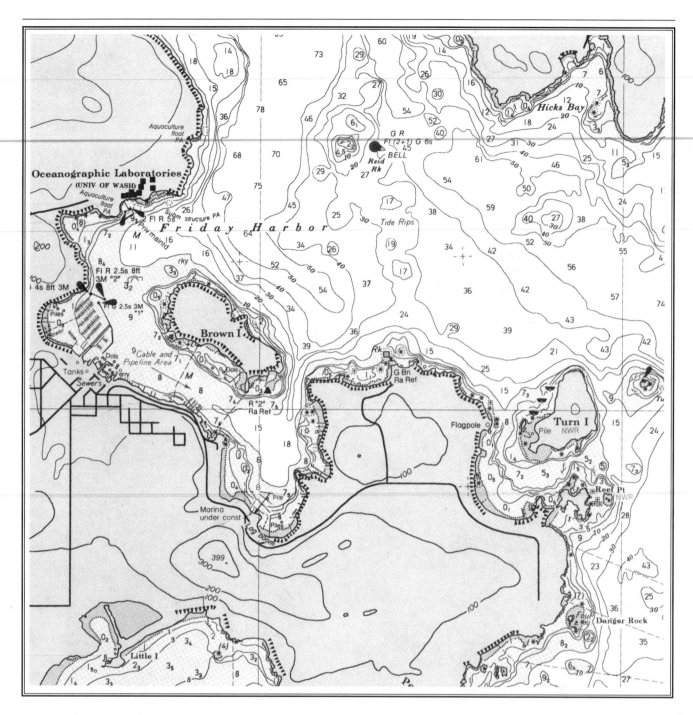

Friday Harbor. Busy summer weekends will find the docks full, and many boats anchored between Brown Island and the town. Good anchorage is available at the south end of Friday Harbor.

Not intended for navigation

The other story is that a survey boat came into the bay. An officer, seeing a man on shore, called out, "What bay is this?" Thinking the officer had asked "What day is this?" the man answered, "Friday," whereupon Friday Bay was put on the charts.

One of Friday Harbor's outstanding features is the University of Washington's Marine Laboratories, which were established in 1903 by the university's prominent biologist, Professor Trevor Kincaid. The Marine Laboratories are used by advanced students in several university departments, and are open to visitors on specific days during the summer.

Friday Harbor looking south, with Dinner Island and Griffin Bay in the background.

Again, for a detailed account of the island's fascinating history, I recommend David Richardson's book *Pig War Islands*. It is interesting reading.

San Juan Island has a dozen or so lakes, and, with the exception of San Juan Valley lying west and southwest of Friday Harbor, the topography is fairly rough. There are several high hills, with Mt. Dallas (at 1,080 feet) topping Cady Mountain (900 feet), Young Hill (680 feet), and several others ranging from 200 to 960 feet. Mt. Dallas was probably named for Alexander Grant Dallas, a director of the Hudson's Bay Company and president of its council in North America, as well as being Governor Douglas's son-in-law. Cady Mountain was named for William and John Cady, two pioneer brothers who lived on the mountain in the 1870's.

The cruising yachtsman's chief interest in San Juan Island lies in the several bays, some of them around the north end of the island, and some along the east shore, facing **San Juan Channel**. The southwestern coast of the island is rugged, most of it is fairly steep, and there are no bays offering good anchorage.

With a little redesigning, San Juan Island could almost resemble a miniature version of North America (in which Griffin Bay would become the Gulf of Mexico). **Cattle Point**, at the southern tip, marks one side of **Middle Channel**, now often called **Cattle Pass**. Again, two stories are told concerning the name. One is that a boatload of cattle from Victoria was wrecked on the rocks and the cattle swam ashore

King's Market in Friday Harbor is a popular shopping destination for visting cruisers. A well-stocked chandlery is upstairs.

to the point. The other holds that the point was frequently used as a place for boats to load and unload cattle.

Salmon Bank, an extensive rocky shoal, extends south from Cattle Point. *With depths from 1½ to 4 fathoms, Salmon Bank should be avoided, particularly in heavy weather or when tide rips are present.* There is an inner passage which can be used with local knowledge. A lighted bell buoy marks the southern extremity of the shoal.

The promontory extending northward from Cattle Point is named Cape San Juan. It is almost cut off from the rest of the island by **Fish Creek**, a narrow finger some 500 yards long. With depths of 1½ to 2 fathoms except at the head, Fish Creek frequently is used as a layover by small craft when the strait is kicking up outside.

Harbor Rock, lying about 200 yards north of the cape, is well marked by surrounding kelp. *Be sure to go around Harbor Rock, not between Harbor Rock and the point.*

Griffin Bay, named for Charles John Griffin, the Hudson's Bay Company official who was in charge of Bellevue Farm in Pig War days, is open to the north and northeast. Above Griffin Bay are **Jensen Bay**, **Mulno Cove**, and **North Bay**. *Rocks are scattered generously along this entire shore, so care should be used.*

Dinner Island, in the south part of North Bay, is said to have been so named because the crew from a British vessel landed there to eat. Another story holds that a pioneer family who lived on the shore behind the island used to row over to shoot rabbits when food supplies ran low.

A large cape topped by 200-foot-high Bald Hill extends east, with **Turn Island** and **Turn Rock** off to the northeast. Wilkes, thinking Turn Island was a point of San Juan Island, named it Point Salsbury for Francis Salsbury, a captain of the top in the expedition. In 1858 the present name of Turn Island was given to mark the turn in the channel. Turn Island is a state marine park with picnic facilities, pit toilets, 10 camp sites, hiking trails, and clams. *If you have never explored the scenic little channel behind Turn Island, you have missed one of the most pleasant small waterways in the islands.* Next time give yourself a treat and try it. Use large-scale chart 18434.

Around the head of the cape is **Friday Harbor**, well protected by **Brown Island**. Wilkes named the island for John G. Brown, a mathematical and nautical instrument maker for the expedition. In recent years real estate developers have called it Friday Island, but it is still officially charted as Brown Island.

Friday Harbor offers good protected anchorage south of Brown Island, and in the cove behind the cape. Moorage can be obtained at the municipal marina floats and at several oil company floats. *At the southern end of the bay are two complete shipyards with full marine services.* The port of Friday Harbor has both temporary and overnight moorage and is located on the west shore. It can accommodate almost 600 boats, including about 130 transient vessels. A slip assignment station is on breakwater A (May to September) and the port stands by on VHF channel 66A for the same purpose. During the summer you can clear customs at the end of the breakwater. Full marine services are available.

The town of Friday Harbor, which is the largest in the islands and serves as the county seat, has all kinds of stores, shops, and markets, banks and restaurants, hotels and medical-dental facilities. Don't miss the Whale Museum one block up Front Street.

Reid Rock, lying about in mid-channel outside the harbor and marked by a lighted bell buoy, was named by Richards, presumably for Captain James Murray Reid of the Hudson's Bay Company.

Out of the harbor and around **Point Caution**, the northeast shore of San Juan Island is fairly steep up to **Rocky Bay. O'Neal Island** lies in the middle of Rocky Bay. A couple of small coves in Rocky Bay offer some protection. *The northeast corner of San Juan Island, around Limestone Point, and the north shore are scalloped with shoals, reefs, and rocks, so do not get in too close.*

Davison Head is anvil shaped and is almost a separate island. **Neil Bay,** formed behind Davison Head, is shallow, shoaling and drying at

Roche Harbor looking southwest. Roche Harbor is one of the most popular stopovers in the islands, and is a U.S. Customs station.

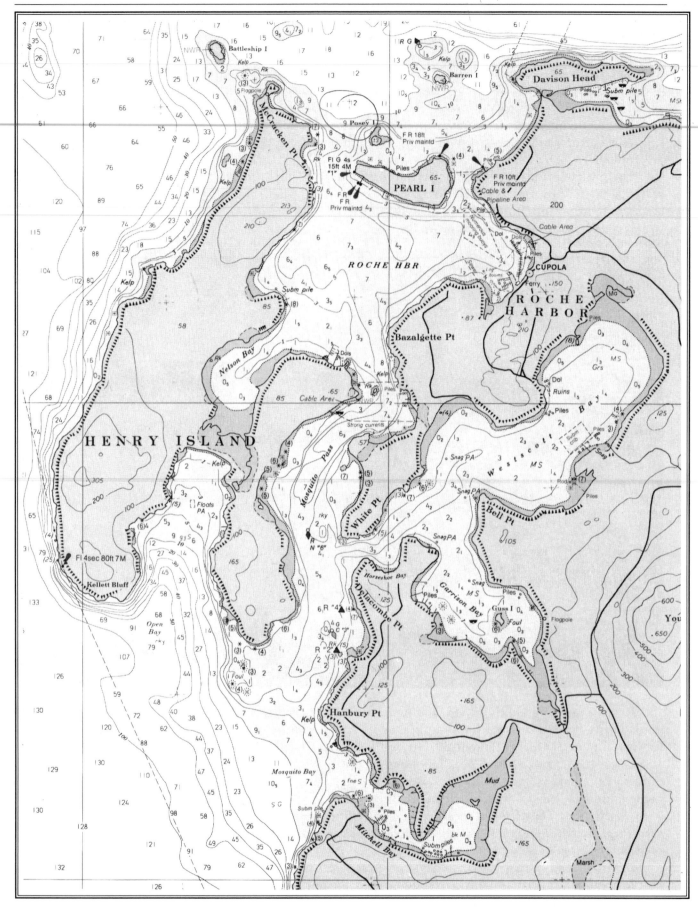

EDEN ARTS

the head and open to the east. Rocks along the north face of Davison Head are marked by kelp; good fishing is usually found there.

Around the western end of Davison Head are little **Barren Island** and **Posey Island**. Both are publicly owned, but only Posey Island can be visited. It has picnic facilities, tables and stoves, pit toilets, and a campsite. Clamming is good on the beaches. Barren Island is a national wildlife refuge, and you may *not* go ashore.

To the south is **Roche Harbor**, protected on the north by **Pearl Island** and on the west by **Henry Island**. Roche Harbor was named by Richards in 1858 for Lieutenant Richard Roche, who served under Kellett in 1846 and under Captain James C. Prevost between 1857 and 1860. A Hudson's Bay Company trading post was established at Roche Harbor in 1850. Roche Harbor later became famous for a lime-producing company, whose history will be found chapter 15. Today the harbor is one of the best-known marine resorts in the islands, and it has every facility for the yachtsman and his family.

From the north, entrance to Roche Harbor usually is made between Henry Island and Pearl Island, although the passage at the eastern end of Pearl Island often is used except during minus tides. *For safety, keep a mid-channel course.*

Roche Harbor provides excellent protected anchorage throughout, with the cove at the western end of Henry Island favored by some skippers. The Seattle Yacht Club has an outstation at Henry Island, and its moorage is for members only. Nelson Bay also can be

Roche Harbor, looking west, with Pearl Island marking the northern entrance.

OPPOSITE: Roche Harbor and surroundings. Roche Harbor is a U.S. Customs Port of Entry. Fuel, a well-stocked store, and a good restaurant are available. Roche Harbor has good anchorage, although it is crowded in the summer. Slow boats should transit Mosquito Pass with fair current only.

Not intended for navigation

used if you do not go too far in. Nelson Bay is shallow and it shoals from the head and out from the shores almost to the middle.

Mosquito Pass, a winding, scenic passage with some shoal areas which are marked with kelp, runs between San Juan Island and Henry Island, and leads from Roche Harbor to Haro Strait. *Stay to the east of little Pole Island near the north end of Mosquito Pass, and then steer a mid-channel course except at the south, where kelp-covered shoals should be passed to the west.* Strong currents can run through Mosquito Pass at times, so be sure to allow for them, particularly in the shoal areas. A study of chart 18433 is recommended, especially at the lower stages of the tide.

Taking off from Mosquito Pass is the channel leading to Westcott Bay and Garrison Bay. **Westcott Bay** trends northwestward, running

The view of Roche Harbor looking southeast. Wescott Bay is to the left in the distance, and Garrison Bay to the right. Henry Island is in the foreground right. The docks are part of the Seattle Yacht Club outstation, and are for members' use only.

EDEN ARTS

up behind the Roche Harbor lime quarries. Westcott Bay is a fine, landlocked haven but is quite shallow. If you anchor in Westcott Bay use the depth sounder or lead line. At low tide the dense growth of eel grass can help locate the shallow areas.

Garrison Bay, so named because British Camp was located there during the Pig War, is another good, protected anchorage if care is taken to watch the depths. **Guss Island**, in the bay, was named for Guss Hoffmaster, who ran a store serving the soldiers at English Camp during the 1850's and 1860's.

EDEN ARTS

View to the Northeast, with the entrances to Wescott Bay to the left of the photo, and Garrison Bay to the right. British Camp can be seen on the shore of Garrison Bay.

The years spent in occupation by British marines on the shores of lovely Garrison Bay are memorialized by several names in the vicinity. **Bazalgette Point**, at the north entrance to Mosquito Pass, was named by Pender for Captain George Bazalgette, a commander of British Camp during some of the Pig War years. **Delacombe Point**, at the channel entering Westcott and Garrison bays, was named for Captain William A. Delacombe, who succeeded Bazalgette as commander of British Camp. **Hanbury Point**, at the southern end of the passage, was named by Pender for Ingham Hanbury, a Royal Navy assistant and surgeon who served at British Camp.

Just below the southern end of Mosquito Pass, **Mitchell Bay** indents San Juan Island easterly for about ⅔ of a mile. Mitchell Bay probably was named by Richards for Captain William Mitchell of the Hudson's Bay Company, who was in charge of the *Beaver*. Mitchell Bay is very shallow, with depths of only 3 to 6 feet at zero tide. It is a beautiful spot, however, and should not be passed by if you want to know these waters. The **Snug Harbor Marina** is on the south shore of Mitchell Bay, just inside the entrance. Except for diesel fuel, it has complete facilities for the yachtsman.

In visiting Mitchell Bay you will feel safer, unless you have a shallow-draft boat, if you go in on a half-tide or better. ***On entering, stay well to the left to avoid the finger shoal extending to about mid-channel from the south.*** The shores shoal out a way, and the head of the inner bay dries at low water. Check large-scale chart 18433 closely to avoid any trouble.

Down San Juan Island's coast a short distance is **Smugglers Cove**, during the smuggling era a favorite spot to land Canadian contraband on American soil. A bit more than 1 mile south, little **Low Island**, lying just offshore, is an undeveloped state marine park. Just below, **Smallpox Bay** (shallow and offering little protection) got its name from the fact that many Indians stricken with smallpox jumped into the icy water there in an effort to rid themselves of fever. Most died of pneumonia.

Henry Island, shaped like a crude *H*, was named by Wilkes for his nephew, Midshipman Wilkes Henry, who was killed by Fiji Island

Mitchell Bay, just south of Mosquito Pass, is shallow, with rocks in the entrance, but with a good chart can be navigated safely.

Battleship Island, off the northern tip of Henry Island, is aptly named.

natives when the expedition stopped there on its way to the Pacific Northwest. **Open Bay** is just what its name implies, but it does offer good anchorage except in southerly winds.

Kellett Bluff, on the southwest tip of San Juan Island, was named for Captain Henry Kellett of the British surveying vessel *Herald*. Kellett, who charted these waters in 1847, named many of the geographic points in the islands. Fishing off the bluff and up Henry Island's west side is usually good for sea bass, cod, and salmon.

Battleship Island, off the northwest tip of Henry Island, was so named because its silhouette, when viewed from certain positions, resembles a battleship. Battleship Island is an undeveloped state marine park.

A word is in order here about these so-called undeveloped state marine parks. With more and more mainland city dwellers acquiring island property for summer homes or permanent residences, small islands and island waterfront property are becoming almost unavailable. This means there are fewer and fewer places for the cruising family to go ashore.

With an eye to the future and recognizing the need for access to the shore, Washington State Parks and Recreation Commission officials are acquiring suitable property for marine parks as funds become available. In the San Juan Islands alone, the state now owns 17 marine parks and more than 42 undeveloped islands, rocks, and reefs. Some will be developed as marine parks as the budget permits. Others will be left undeveloped.

The yachtsman, if he knows where these properties are located, can feel free to go ashore for exploring, rock or driftwood hunting, camping, picnicking, clamming, skin diving, or hiking, with the knowledge that he is not trespassing on private property. Boat owners and their families should be thankful for this far-sighted program. A complete list of state marine parks can be obtained by writing the Washington State Parks and Recreation Commission, 7150 Clearwater Lane KY-11, Olympia, WA 98504-5711, or you can call (206) 753-2027 and give them your address. The information is free.

C H A P T E R

13

LOPEZ ISLAND

Hughes Bay on the south end of
Lopez Island, with the entrance to
McArdle Bay in the background.

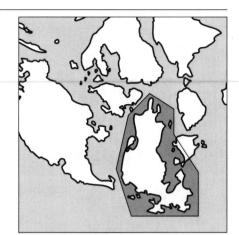

Of the larger islands in the San Juans group, Lopez Island is probably the least known to yachtsmen, most of whom are acquainted only with its shores and a few of its bays. Lopez Island is an evergreen-clad, insular paradise exuding its own brand of magic. Third largest of the San Juans, Lopez Island's 54-square-mile area places it only slightly behind Orcas Island and San Juan Island in size. Lopez Island has almost no local industry. The permanent residents—many of them descended from original settlers—engage mostly in farming, cattle raising, and fishing.

Years ago the farms and orchards of Lopez Island produced phenomenal crops, dairies set records, and fishing was so good that canneries often could not keep up with the catch. Today a shifting economy has made these pursuits less lucrative. However, many island people seem not to be unduly concerned with monetary riches. Their wealth is of another kind, a close-to-nature life with fewer of the pressures of urban society.

The village of Lopez, the only major settlement, is located at the entrance to Fisherman Bay on the island's west side. A few stores in much smaller communities are scattered around the island. The island has some summer homes, and in recent years it has become a vacation favorite of many Boeing employees.

History does not seem to agree on just who was Lopez Island's first permanent white settler. James Nelson, a Danish sailor, claimed no one living on Lopez Island when he settled there in 1862. However, a settler named Davis is recorded as having a run-in with soldiers from Camp Pickett in 1865, and the name Davis Bay appears on British charts of 1859. Arthur ("Billy") Barlow was another resident who settled on the south end of the island in the early days.

More settlers arrived in 1869 and 1870, including one Hiram Hutchinson, who set up a store where the village of Lopez is now located.

The first real argument as to whether the San Juan Islands were owned by Britain or the United States is believed to have occurred on Lopez Island. Richard Cussans, an American, was on Lopez Island cutting quantities of its tall, strong, and straight timber as spars for San Francisco sailing ships. Sir James Douglas, the newly-named governor of Vancouver Island, promptly informed Cussans that he

Flat Point
Fisherman Bay
Goose Island
Deadman Island
Whale Rocks
Mummy Rocks
Davis Bay
Richardson
Jones Bay
Mackaye Harbor
Aleck Bay
Hughes Bay
McArdle Bay
Watmough Bay
Swifts Bay
Lopez Sound
Hunter Bay
Spencer Spit

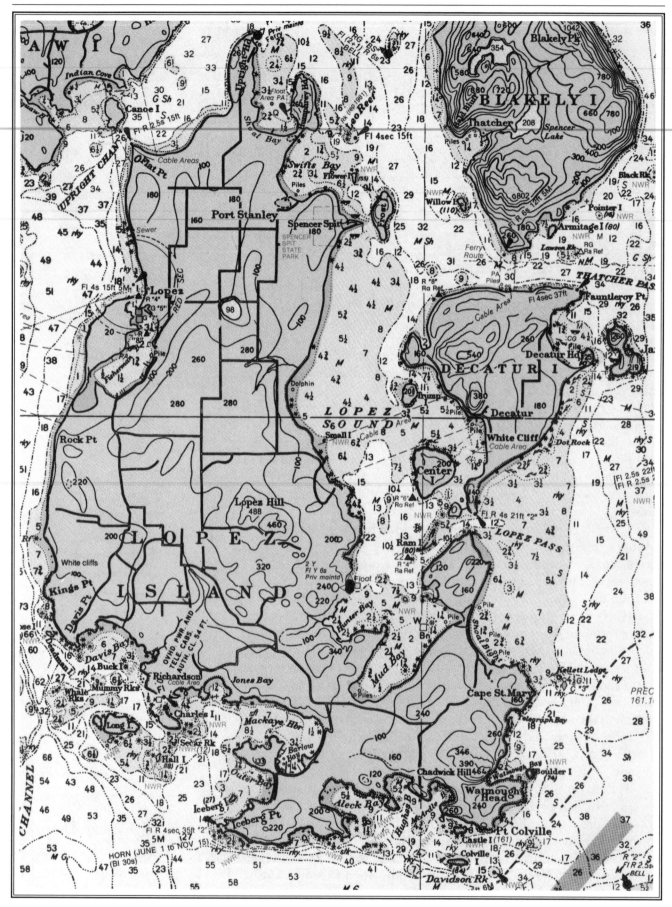

Spencer Spit is unmistakable, and a popular place to anchor or tie off to a mooring buoy. The pass between the spit and Frost Island is narrow but deep.

was trespassing on British property and should "cease and desist." Cussans stayed on and Douglas sent a party to the island to claim it formally for Her Majesty's government. This incident reportedly occurred in 1853 and predated the Pig War on San Juan Island, recounted in Chapter 11.

Early days on Lopez Island were not without their moments of violence. Old-timers still tell the story of an argument over a cow between Swedish John Anderson and Norwegian John Kay. The argument ended in a fight, during which Kay shot Anderson with a pistol at close range. Kay was convicted of second-degree murder, but served only a short part of his 10-year sentence in the federal prison on Washington's McNeil Island.

Another tragic shooting, this one more or less accidental, occurred a few years later. A young bridegroom, tired of a shivaree being staged by his friends, sought to discourage them by firing a double-barrel shotgun over their heads. The twin blasts were not aimed high enough and two of his friends were hit. After three days of frustrating attempts to get medical help through stormy seas to Lopez Island, one of the victims died. The other victim lingered three years with a pellet in his spine before succumbing. The young bridegroom was charged with murder, but was acquitted.

It is said that the true art of ferryboat skippering was born in the San Juan Islands, and one of the most skillful of the early-day captains was Sam Barlow of Lopez Island. Barlow began his seagoing career at the age of three, when he and one of his brothers decided to take a cruise in a canoe. Fortunately, an older sister saw the boys leaving and cancelled their trip. Sam spent much of his youth learning all the San Juan channels and passages with their rocks and reefs. By the time Sam was old enough to get his master's papers, he had an intimate

OPPOSITE: Lopez Island. Fisherman Bay is open and inviting, but the south end of the island is sobering. Mackaye Harbor is a popular overnight for boats planning an early-morning jump across the strait to Port Townsend. Lopez Sound is beautiful and often overlooked.

Not intended for navigation

133

Looking southeast across Lopez Island. Decatur Island is left center; Shaw Island is at the bottom of the photo; Lopez Island is in the center; other San Juan Islands are in the background.

knowledge of the island waters and probably could have navigated them blindfolded.

Like other inland-water skippers, Captain Sam developed an ability to determine his position from echoes of his ship's whistle as they bounced off a hillside or a rock cliff. Using this method, Sam could find his distance offshore just as surely as if he had plotted it on a chart. It is said that, in a heavy fog, he would exchange his skipper's cap for a broad-brimmed felt hat, which permitted him to hear the echoes better. As a further aid, Sam's sense of smell was reputed to be so keen he could detect the odor of kelp at a considerable distance and so keep clear of dangerous rocks.

Captain Sam, with his talents and experience, came to be known as the dean of ferry boat skippers. He logged some 20,000 trips over 47 years without serious accident.

Lopez Island was named for Lopez Gonzales de Haro, a pilot, sailing master, and first mate for Eliza. Haro Strait was also named for de Haro, who, with Ensign Manuel Quimper, was one of the first Europeans to see the San Juan Islands, although at a considerable distance from aboard his ship.

History is vague as to just when the name Lopez was first given to this island. Wilkes, in 1841, called it Chauncey's Island, for Commodore Isaac Chauncey, the commander of U.S. forces on the Great Lakes in the War of 1812. What we know as Lopez Sound was named Macedonian Crescent by Wilkes, for the British frigate captured by Captain Stephen Decatur.

Kellett either gave or restored the name Lopez to the island in 1847. The U.S. Coast Survey changed the names of the sound and channel in 1854.

The ferry landing on Lopez Island is at **Upright Head**, the island's northern tip. Cruising down **Upright Channel**, **Flat Point** seems to point a finger across the channel at **Canoe Island**. Flat Point, with its few trees standing straight and tall like sentinels, is one of the most frequently photographed spots in the San Juan archipelago.

About 1¾ miles below Flat Point is the entrance to **Fisherman Bay**, as delightful a harbor as one could visit. For the first-timer, this entrance, tucked behind a finger spit, can be hard to find. There are, however, at least two ways to locate it easily. One way, if coming from the north, is to cruise as close as possible to shore from Flat Point, being careful to stay outside the rocks scattered offshore. *It is best to stay 150 to 200 yards out, making it easy to pick up the markers at the entrance to the bay.*

A second method is recommended by Lloyd Vosper. Vosper's *Cruising Puget Sound and Adjacent Waters* unfortunately is out of print, but in that book, Vosper says:

> … use a range between Turn Rock and the small white church on Lopez Island. This should clear the sand bar which extends in a northerly direction from the end of the sandspit. The end of the spit is step-to allowing passage close aboard.

Once inside Fisherman Bay, the channel to the main bay is well marked and these markers should be carefully heeded to avoid the shoal areas. Safe and pleasant anchorage can be found in the small coves inside the entrance, although most skippers prefer to anchor in the main bay or tie up at the floats of the **Islander Lopez Resort**.

This resort, formerly known as Pantley's Resort and before that as the Ebb Tide Resort and Lopez Inn, has moorage for 50 boats, and offers a complete range of marina facilities and services. The heated swimming pool and hot tub are surrounded by shoreside game areas, so this is a popular spot for the whole crew. There are guest units, and a rustic main lodge, dining room, and cocktail lounge with entertainment, all done in Polynesian decor. In the summer reservations are recommended. Also located in Fisherman Bay, next to the Islander Lopez, is **Islands Marine Center**, with marine parts, services, and repairs, transient and long-term moorage for boats, haulouts to 15 tons, boat sales, fishing tackle, and showers. The center monitors channel 69 VHF for reservations.

Because of the low strip of land across the southwest end of the bay, strong winds sometimes blow through from that direction, but the area is sufficiently confined that objectionable seas do not build up. All told, Fisherman Bay is a most pleasant place to visit, and the sun, setting behind the trees on the outer peninsula, presents a picture not soon forgotten.

Either because of its apparent exposure to the furies of a sometimes boisterous strait or the navigational hazards of its rock-strewn

Fisherman Bay, showing the narrow entrance. The village of Lopez, with shopping, is opposite the entrance. The larger of the two docks is Islands Marine Center, and the smaller is the Islander Lopez.

EDEN ARTS

waters, the southern end of Lopez Island has never been extremely popular with Northwest yachtsmen. This is unfortunate. A stern, rugged beauty is to be found in the many bays, coves, and beaches. It is a landscape not found anywhere else in the islands. A spirit of adventure and daring as well as plenty of caution are required to make the trip, but the skipper who adds this area to his cruising itinerary will be richly rewarded.

Of course, it is wise to choose a day when the winds are calm. Preferably, it should be a sunny day and there should be a good supply of film aboard, for the possibilities for the photographer are many and spectacular.

The approach from the north is from San Juan Channel, through **Cattle Pass** between **Goose Island** and **Deadman Island**. Deadman Island actually was given away as first prize in a radio contest some years ago. The winning essay had to do with the joys of living on an island, but apparently the writer did not convince herself. She promptly traded her island for a car.

In my own exploration of the bays and coves along the southern coast of Lopez Island, I first made a careful study of large-scale chart 18434. *A bow lookout, depth sounder, and slow, slow speed are essential, at least until the skipper is well acquainted here.* Carefully watching **Whale Rocks**, I went midway between **Mummy Rocks** and **Davis Point** to miss the rock off Davis Point, and then into **Davis Bay**. The shore is shoal and lined with rocks, and the bay is quite exposed. Slowed almost to a drift, I passed **Buck Island** to the west, ran between **Long Island** and **Charles Island**, and kept little **Hall Island** fairly close to starboard to avoid **Secar Rock**. I did not quite dare to try the passage in back of Charles Island, but perhaps I shall another time.

A course slightly to the right of mid-channel between Charles Island and **John's Point** to the east gives a clear entrance to **Richardson**, **Jones Bay**, **Mackaye Harbor**, and **Barlow Bay**, which was named for the pioneer Barlow family. Here are scenic protected waters with good depths and very few hazards. The docks and floats in Barlow Bay are privately owned or restricted to fishing boats.

Richardson, the southernmost community on Lopez Island, was a busy place in pioneer days. Richardson was named for George Richardson, the community's first settler, who arrived in 1871. It had

The Richardson store is no more. Here is how it looked before it burned.

DAVE CALHOUN

138

one of the island's early post offices, and a large two-story hall, which served as church, school, dance hall, and social center. As a port, Richardson was the first island landing for steamers serving the islands from Seattle by way of Port Townsend. It was an unloading center for the countless fishing boats that took advantage of the tremendous salmon fishing enjoyed around the turn of the century.

Visiting Richardson today, it is hard to visualize the great activity there nearly a century ago, when more than 400 men fished the surrounding waters and their boats crowded the harbor. The present and only store, located across the street from the site of the original shop, is a typical rural general store out of the past. One can buy groceries, hardware, dry goods, or even an ice cream cone to top off a visit. Recently, the store was added to the ranks of the National Register of Historical Places, and has the only dock with diesel fuel on Lopez Island.

Editor's Note: As this edition was being prepared for the press, word was received that on October 27, 1990 the Richardson Store burned to the ground. The store was not rebuilt, but fuel is available during limited hours. Moorage is alongside high pilings and difficult for pleasurecraft. The above description and accompanying photo are included as a reminder of what used to be.

Looking north across the south end of Lopez Island. The docks can be seen jutting into Barlow Bay, with Lopez Sound in the background.

EDEN ARTS

Mackaye Harbor, with **Barlow Bay** nestled along its south shore, is a popular anchorage for boats planning an early morning trip across the Strait of Juan de Fuca. Westerly winds from the strait often send a steady stream of rollers into Mackaye Harbor, but the holding ground is good. You can find protection from most of the action by anchoring in Barlow Bay. If you anchor outside of Barlow Bay, in Mackaye Harbor, *be sure the anchor is well set and pay out ample scope, and you will get through the night without trouble*. Around John's Point from Barlow Bay and Mackaye Harbor is **Outer Bay**. Open to westerly winds, its fine gravel beach is piled high with drift logs.

Running behind **Iceberg Island** in Outer Bay, I rounded **Iceberg Point**. Iceberg Point was named by the U.S. Coast Survey in 1854 because of what surveyors called "the remarkable deep and smooth markings of glacial action." Following the ten-fathom lines carefully, we made the tricky entrance between Iceberg Point and **Swirl Island**, then around **Aleck Rocks** into **Aleck Bay**. Aleck Bay and its neighbors **Hughes Bay** and **McArdle Bay**, with their generous scattering of islands, isles, and rocks, display an almost never-ending series of sensationally rugged vistas. This trio of bays, with beaches and coves

Lopez Island, south end. Rocks and strong westerly winds can require careful boat handling, but the rugged coast is worth exploring.

Not intended for navigation

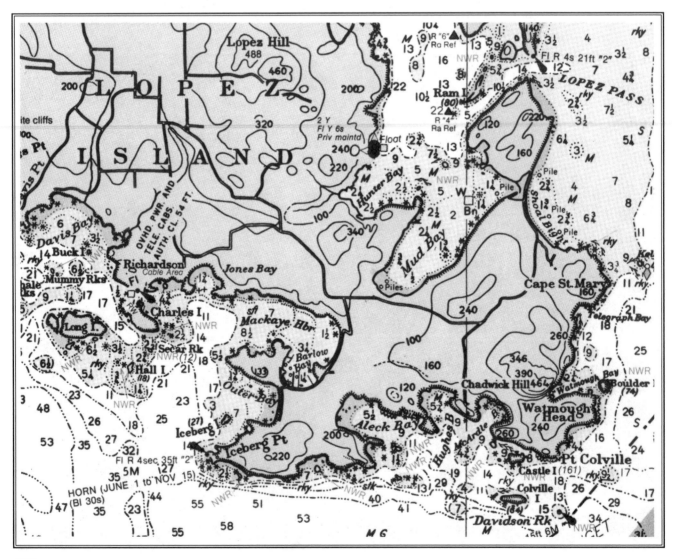

framed by trees twisted by the sea wind, is exposed to both southwest and southeast winds, but is well worth waiting out the weather to see.

To the southeast, just outside Aleck Bay, **Castle Island**, **Colville Island**, and **Davidson Rock** stand guard. Formidable Castle Island, given its descriptive name by British Admiralty charts of 1859-60, was named Old Hundred Island by the U.S. Coast Survey of 1855. Colville Island and Point Colville were named for Andrew Colville, the governor of the Hudson's Bay Company from 1852 to 1856. Davidson Rock, originally called Entrance Rock by the Coast Survey, was named by Richards to honor Captain George Davidson of the U.S. Coast Survey, who explored the charted Northwest waters in the late 1850's. **Watmough Head** and **Watmough Bay**, on the southeastern tip of Lopez Island, were named by Wilkes, probably for the Lieutenant John Goddard Watmough of the U.S. Army, who was wounded at Fort Erie in the Niagara Campaign of 1814.

The east side of Lopez Island, facing on **Lopez Sound**, has a number of interesting features. On the north end, between **Upright Head** and **Humphrey Head**, is **Shoal Bay**. Despite its name, Shoal Bay is shoal only a short distance out from its shores; depths are from 9 to 21 feet at zero tide. Below Shoal Bay and around Humphrey Head is **Swifts Bay**, guarded by **Leo Reef** and rocky **Flower Island**. The shores of Swifts Bay also shoal out and have rocks in places. While depths are from 12 to 20 feet, there is not much protection.

Lopez Island history is interesting. In 1892, efforts were made to start a town by one Frank P. Baum, an attorney turned newspaper publisher and editor in Friday Harbor. Baum had been unsuccessful in his campaign against the immorality of saloons in Friday Harbor, so he moved his San Juan County *Graphic* to Lopez Island. Soon Baum became captivated with the idea of starting a new town, a town in which there would be churches, morals, and no saloons. With several partners and high hopes Baum organized a real estate company and bought property around the lagoon off Swifts Bay.

Baum named the new town Port Stanley, for Sir Henry Stanley, the British explorer and author. Port Stanley began with a combined store and post office, as well as the publishing and editorial offices of the *Graphic*. The dream had a short life, however. The depression of 1893 defeated all of Baum's great plans.

EDEN ARTS

Outer Bay, with Iceberg Island in the mouth, looks calm in this photo, but is open to rollers from summertime westerlies in the Strait of Juan de Fuca.

To the southeast of Swifts Bay lies **Spencer Spit**, a state marine park that stabs at **Frost Island**. Spencer Spit has 12 mooring buoys, 30 standard tent sites, restrooms, a trailer dump facility, and a log picnic shelter. This sandy finger is fine for picnicking or camping if the wind is not too strong. Wilkes named Frost Island for John Frost, a boatswain on the *Porpoise*. The spit acquired its name from the Spencer family, who owned it for many years before it became a park.

At the south end, or head, of Lopez Sound are Hunter Bay and Mud Bay. **Hunter Bay** offers a good protected anchorage in at least 2 fathoms and is a favorite haven of many cruising families. **Mud Bay** has a minimum depth of 4 feet at low tide, shoaling shores, and some rocks and pilings, so is not much used for anchorage. However, Mud Bay is fun to explore at higher stages of the tide or by dinghy at lower tides if one watches for the rocks. Scenic rewards are plentiful.

If any skipper is interested in adding some local names of little islets in the area to his chart, the small dot just north of the point separating Hunter Bay and Mud Bay is called **Crab Island**. Northeast, a larger island, lying a short distance off the mouth of a cove on the inside of the Lopez Island toe, is named **Fortress Island**, while the islet in the entrance to the same cove is another **Skull Island**.

West of this lower end of Lopez Sound, the wooded hills of the Lopez Range rise to a maximum height of 480 feet at Lopez Hill, called by some Mt. Lopez. This is considerably less than the more rugged heights found on Orcas Island and San Juan Island.

Even though the cruising yachtsman may not find too much of interest on Lopez Island itself, the island magic is very much in evidence all around its shores. Lopez Island definitely is a lovely part of this constellation of islands.

A look at Alec Rocks and Alec Bay.

EDEN ARTS

Humphrey Head, at the northeast corner of Lopez Island, helps form Shoal Bay.

Swifts Bay (left) and Shoal Bay (lower right) are at the northeast corner of Lopez Island.

14

THE FOUR MIDDLE PASSES

Boulders seem to erupt from the waters off a
point on the inside of James Island

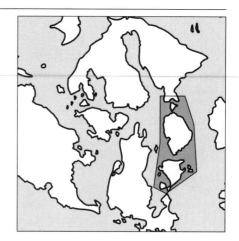

Buffering the San Juans to the west of a sometimes angry Rosario Strait are a couple of the larger islands and a half-dozen or so of their satellites. Four passages, each with its own character, separate the islands. These evergreen islands, surrounded by the sparkling waters of this cruising paradise, hold an important place both historically and esthetically in the archipelago of the San Juans.

Obstruction Island, where there has been some real estate development in recent years, acts as a sort of traffic divider between **Obstruction Pass** to the north and **Peavine Pass** to the south. **Peavine Pass**, the shorter of the two, is clear of dangers with plenty of depth. *Rocks south of the eastern entrance to Peavine Pass are marked with a beacon. Currents can attain velocities of 3 to 4 knots in the pass, and, on occasion, the skipper will encounter tide rips outside.*

South of Peavine Pass is **Blakely Island**, sometimes called the Paradise Isle and referred to by some as the Flying Island. Blakeley Island was named by Wilkes for Johnston Blakely, the commander of the U.S. sloop of war *Wasp* in the War of 1812. Judging from the kitchen middens (ancient mounds of discarded clam and oyster shells) still in evidence, Indians were living on Blakely Island for some time. With the arrival of the white man, the island contributed still more to the colorful history of the area. There are remnants of two old gold mines and a deteriorating schoolhouse. Records of a neighborhood quarrel and murder are part of Blakely Island's past.

Blakely Island is rugged, with several high hills topped by 1,060-foot-high Blakely Peak. Much of the natural beauty of the island remains untouched by development. Wildlife is abundant; there are plenty of minks, racoons, seals, otters, game animals, and birds, and one of the largest herds of tame deer in the country. There are some 17 miles of beaches and cliff-rimmed shores, as well as two beautiful lakes. Spencer Lake offers the fisherman both large- and small-mouth bass, and Horseshoe Lake has trout.

Paul Hubbs, the vagabond of the San Juans, seems to have been the first recorded white man on Blakely Island, although he was not really a permanent resident. From his home on Orcas Island, Hubbs used Blakely Island to run a herd of sheep. The first permanent settler, apparently, was E. C. Gillette, who figured in San Juan Islands affairs in several capacities.

Blakely and Decatur Islands.

Not intended for navigation

EDEN ARTS

In 1889 Richard H. Straub bought Gillette's spread on Blakely Island and later became the island's schoolteacher. In a series of unfortunate events, Straub was fired, his wife died suddenly, and Straub became embroiled in an argument with neighbors. Straub shot Leon Lanterman, a relative of the neighbors, who was visiting from Decatur Island. After considerable excitement and a threatened lynching, Straub was tried, found guilty of first-degree murder, and in 1897 hanged at Friday Harbor.

When Floyd Johnson bought Blakely Island in 1954, he dreamed of retaining its primitive beauty for the enjoyment of a select group

Obstruction Pass, between Obstruction Island and Orcas Island, takes a dogleg shape, but presents no navigation problems.

1 Shaw Island; 2 Indian Cove; 3 Obstruction Island; 4 Cypress Island; 5 Blakely Island;
6 Guemes Island; 7 Lopez Island; 8 Anacortes; 9 Decatur Island; 10 Fisherman Bay

ABOVE: The Blakely Island Marina has moorage in
its small-craft basin and at dockside.

BELOW: Peavine Pass lies between Blakely Island
and Obstruction Island. The Blakely Island
Marina can be seen to the right.

of boating and flying enthusiasts. Instead of developing and selling as many sites as he could and attracting as many people as possible, Johnson sought only a minimum number of buyers with whom to share this last frontier. Every effort has been made by its property owners to keep the island's roads, trails, forests, and lakes in their original state.

For flying enthusiasts, there is a 2,400-foot lighted landing strip with clear approaches over water at both ends. Homes line the strip so that many flyers can park their planes in their own yards.

A complete marina, offering full facilities and services for yachtsmen, is at the north end of Blakely Island, just off the western end of Peavine Pass. A fuel float and temporary moorage in the outer bay is available to yachtsmen shopping at the excellent store there. Regular moorage both for island residents and visiting boats is found in the landlocked basin behind the store. The entrance channel to the inner harbor is narrow and shallow, but marked. Even at zero tide the channel will accommodate most boats, with the exception of those with deep draft. Any skipper who is in doubt should ask at the fuel float. The marina, established and run for many years by the late Baylis Harris, is now owned by a partnership of Thomas B. Crowley and Peter Taggares. Moorage reservations are recommended in the summer.

Blakely Island's shores are mostly straight and steep. On the west side is a little bay with 6 to 9 feet of depth offering some protection, but the shores are posted against landing. One-half mile below this bay is **Willow Island**, which can be passed safely on the inside. Around the southern tip, off the southeastern shore of Blakely Island, is

Thatcher Pass, between Decatur Island and Blakely Island, is wide open and easy to navigate.

Decatur Head, with James Island
in the background.

Armitage Island, which stands guard over a couple of small coves that offer some protection.

Thatcher Pass, separating Blakely Island and Decatur Island, is the widest of the four passages. Thatcher Pass is clear of hazards, except for Lawson Rock on the north side of the channel at the eastern entrance. This rock, marked by a buoy, was probably named for a Lieutenant Lawson, who was with the U.S. Coast Survey working in the area around 1852. *When the tide is ebbing against a southerly wind, there can be tide rips off the eastern entrance to Thatcher Pass. Caution should be observed.*

The bay inside Decatur Head, on Decatur Island.

Although Decatur Island has nothing to offer the yachtsman ashore, it is a beautiful island and provides a couple of anchorages. Lower than Blakely Island to the north, Decatur Island's highest point is only 540 feet. Decatur Island was named by Wilkes for Stephen Decatur, a U.S. Navy hero who achieved fame by burning the U.S. frigate *Philadelphia* after it had been captured by Barbary pirates in 1804. British Admiral Lord Nelson called it the most daring feat of

the age. Decatur is also remembered as the author of the patriotic quotation, "Our country: In her intercourse with foreign nations may she always be in the right; but our country, right or wrong!"

Nestled behind a peninsula, with a hump that forms the westernmost point of Decatur Island in Lopez Sound, is one of my favorite coves. Known locally as **Kan Kut Harbor**, the cove is only about 500 yards long by 200 yards wide, with 2 fathoms of depth. For slower boats coming from or returning to mid-Puget Sound, Kan Kut Harbor affords good anchorage for the night. However, if your crew includes a dog requiring a walk, it is better to forget this one; the shores are all privately owned.

A bit to the south is 30-acre **Trump Island**, which can be safely passed on the inside. Although exposed to southerly winds, a small bight on Decatur Island, to the northeast of Trump Island, sometimes is used for anchoring. Still farther south is larger **Center Island**. A broad sandy shelf connects Center Island with Decatur Island, but the water has a least depth of 2 fathoms at zero tide, so safe passage on the inside can be made by keeping in mid-channel. A rock nearly in the channel is buoyed, and other dangers are kelp covered. A fair anchorage can be had in the bight on Decatur Island, west of White Cliff and northeast of Center Island, but a southeast wind blowing across Decatur Island's low southern neck can make it uncomfortable.

Lopez Pass, the closest gate to the western San Juans from Deception Pass, is between Decatur Island and the northern tip of Lopez Island's toe. Though not as clear as the other passages, Lopez Pass can still be negotiated safely if courses are carefully plotted. The easiest and safest course is to turn left after coming through the pass, to run between the

The little bay on the east side of James Island has good anchorage, although open to the wakes of passing ships.

This bay on the west side of James Island looks good, but is subject to strong currents. If anchored, be sure the hook is well set and will not come out if veered.

Lopez Island toe and **Ram Island**. *Be sure to continue on this course far enough to clear the rock that lies about 200 yards off the southern tip of Ram Island.*

The alternative shorter course, used by most skippers after they have tried it a time or two, is a continuation of the course through the pass. There is a rocky islet just north of Ram Island, and another, smaller, rock islet about 100 yards in a line to the north. By aiming dead center between these two islets easy passage can be made, even if it does not look too inviting on the chart.

Lopez Pass, looking north.

On Decatur Island's eastern side is an "almost" island called **Decatur Head**, connected by a low, sandy neck that forms a bay on its north side. The water is shallow, shoaling to about 4 feet off the shore, but affords fair anchorage except in southerly or strong northeast winds.

Close by, to the east of Decatur Head, is **James Island**, a state marine park. Shaped roughly like an hourglass, James Island is lovely and wooded. One mooring buoy and a dock with a small landing float are located in the inner, or western cove. The eastern cove has one mooring buoy. The float is by far the preferred moorage on the west side of James Island, because of the strong currents that run there. If you anchor, be sure your hook has a good bite. The cove on the east side is protected from most winds, but open to the wakes of passing freighter traffic. If you don't mind a little rolling during the night, the eastern cove is a good anchorage.

The passage between Decatur Head and James Island is delightfully scenic, but *be sure to steer a mid-channel course at the southern entrance to clear two rocks, one just off Decatur Head and the other off the point of James Island*. Fishing is usually good in the tide rips north of James Island and on its east side.

James Island was named by Wilkes in connection with Decatur Island but it is not entirely clear for whom it was named. While Stephen Decatur was making his daring effort to burn the *Philadelphia* following its capture by Barbary pirates his brother James was killed. During the ensuing fight, an American sailor named Reuben James saved Decatur's life. Although there might be some question as to which man Wilkes intended to honor, authorities generally agree that it was Reuben James for whom James Island was named.

Whatever the source of its name, James Island is worth the yachtsman's time and should not be bypassed by visitors wanting to achieve full enjoyment of cruising in these waters around the San Juans.

Lopez Pass looks forbidding on the charts, but with attention to the charts can be negotiated quite easily.

James Island

15

TOURING ROCHE HARBOR

Roche Harbor is one of the most
visited stops in the San Juan Islands.

EDEN ARTS

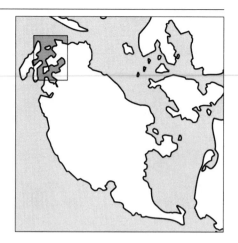

Facilities
History

W hether it is a first cruise to the San Juan Islands, or one of many, really doesn't matter. Cruising the islands is always enjoyable, regardless of how many times one has made the trip. There is infinite variety in the San Juan waterways and islands.

After exploring some of the scenic channels and passages, dropping anchor for a few nights in quiet little coves or bays, it is time for a change. Ship's stores need replenishing. Laundry is to be done, showers to be taken, legs to be stretched, and the mate needs relief from galley duty. Now is the time to stop at Roche Harbor on San Juan Island.

Head west in **Spieden Channel** past the rockbound face of **Davison Head**, swing left around the kelp-covered reef with **Barren Island** to starboard, and enter **Roche Harbor** through the narrow channel between **Pearl Island** and **Government Point**. Throttles are slowed for the search for a moorage at the floats. A courteous, helpful dock boy takes the lines and assists in getting the boat properly secured at the float.

You have arrived! Younger crew members head for the Olympic-sized, heated swimming pool, while the captain and mate stroll up the float toward shore. Although visitors are probably already under the spell of the islands, an additional headiness usually settles over them as they pass through the spectacular formal gardens between the shore and the Hotel de Haro.

Pause in the lobby after making dinner reservations, and look at the old hotel register showing the signature of President Theodore Roosevelt, who occupied room 10 on July 13, 1906. Some years later, President William Howard Taft also visited Roche Harbor. On the lobby walls are pictures showing the company town and some of the activities that contributed to its history.

Before going on to the shore, pick up some descriptive brochures, buy one or two of the island historical books, and buy some postcards, which you can write and post at the hotel while checking for any mail being held for you.

Return to the waterfront and stroll the length of the floats, chatting with old friends and making new ones. Then it is time to go back to the boat for a lazy afternoon sunbath on deck and some reading about the colorful past of this fascinating place.

It was in 1872, at the end of the boundary dispute, that Joe Ruff started it all. He took out a homestead claim on an area around Roche Harbor, where, during the Pig War occupation, British marines at British Camp had set up crude kilns to produce lime. A few years later, Ruff sold out to Robert and Richard Scurr, two brothers who had served with the marines. The Scurr brothers made a small but serious start turning out lime from the large deposits in the hill above the harbor.

Meanwhile, John Stafford McMillin, a young lawyer from Indiana, had become associated with the Tacoma Lime Company. McMillin came to the islands around 1885 to search for limestone deposits the company could buy for expansion. Quick to recognize the potential for Roche Harbor, with its huge hill of purest limestone and a harbor with sufficient depths to accommodate oceangoing ships, McMillin bought the property from the Scurr brothers and formed the Tacoma and Roche Harbor Lime Company.

McMillin, or John S as he was called, was an ardent Republican, a life-long Methodist, a member and later grand consul of Sigma Chi fraternity, and a 32nd-degree Mason. He was dynamic and ambitious, qualities that soon elevated him to the presidency of the company. Confidant of presidents, advisor to government officials, delegate to Republican territorial, county, state, and national conventions, railway commissioner, and almost elected a U.S. senator (he was defeated by a very small margin), McMillin acquired wealth and great prestige.

DAVE CALHOUN

These are the remains of the Scurr Brothers' cabin. The building has deteriorated noticably in the years since this book was first published, in 1973.

Although his public life was important to him, John S put equal, or even more, time and energy into his business. He built the company into the largest lime producer west of the Mississippi, turning out the finest, purest lime at the rate of 1,500 barrels a day. By 1929 the company had a net worth of well over a million dollars.

Roche Harbor lime was shipped all over the world, some of it going to San Francisco for its rebuilding after the 1906 earthquake.

DAVE CALHOUN

The Hotel de Haro is a fixture of Roche Harbor. The path from the docks to the hotel leads through beautiful flower gardens.

Many ships called at Roche Harbor for lime cargoes, and the company operated its own fleet, including three large sailing vesssels, the *Star of Chile*, the *Archer*, and the *William G. Irwin*. It also had five barges and the steam tug *Roche Harbor*, whose moldering hulk can still be seen on the beach, not far from the swimming pool.

For visiting friends and businessmen, McMillin built the Hotel de Haro around the old Hudson's Bay Company post. Adjacent to the hotel he built a banquet court, with two large fireplaces that were used to roast or barbecue sumptuous feasts for his guests. The fireplaces can still be seen, one of them bearing the inscription, "Friendship's fires are always burning."

It was only natural that a town should develop around such an operation. There were a store, school, church, cemetery, offices, a

Roche Harbor has ample transient moorage.

huge warehouse, docks, piers, ship repair yard, and, later, the Bellevue Poultry Farm, established by John S to breed prize-winning fowl and rabbits and to supply food for the kitchens. There were rows of small houses for the families of workers. (Some of the houses are in use today as rental cottages.) The single men lived in bunkhouses along a road behind the church. Japanese workers had their own community around a small cove below the hill on the west end.

At the height of the lime operation, Roche Harbor had a population of nearly 800. It was a company town, embodying the

DAVE CALHOUN

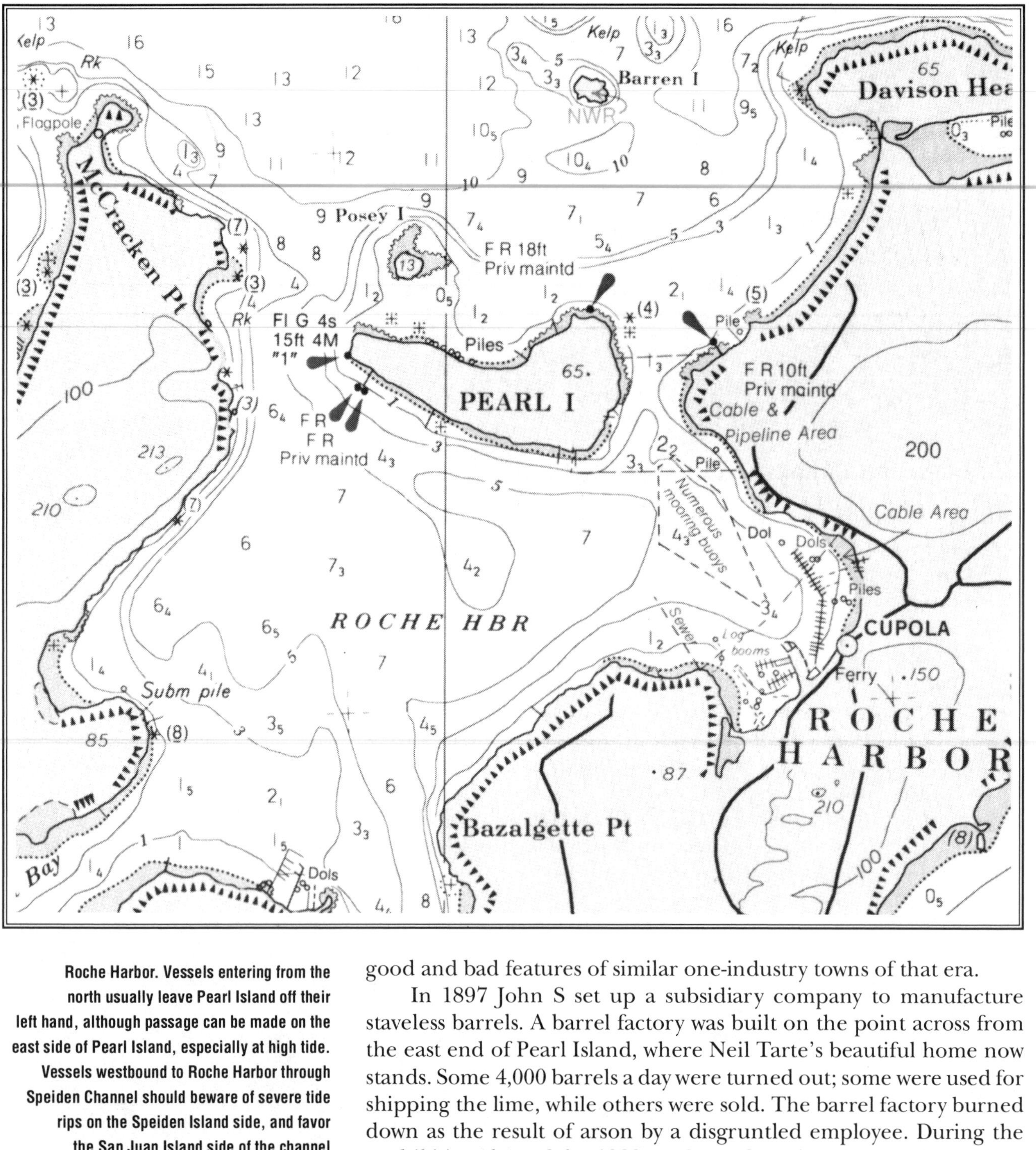
Kelp
Rk
Flagpole
McCracken Pt
Barren I
NWR
Davison Hea
Pile
Posey I
F R 18ft
Priv maintd
Fl G 4s
15ft 4M
"1"
Piles
PEARL I
F R
F R
Priv maintd
F R 10ft
Priv maintd
Cable &
Pipeline Area
Pile
Cable Area
Numerous mooring buoys
Dol
Dols
Piles
CUPOLA
Sewer
Log booms
Ferry
ROCHE HBR
Subm pile
ROCHE
HARBOR
Bazalgette Pt
Bay
Dols

Roche Harbor. Vessels entering from the north usually leave Pearl Island off their left hand, although passage can be made on the east side of Pearl Island, especially at high tide. Vessels westbound to Roche Harbor through Speiden Channel should beware of severe tide rips on the Speiden Island side, and favor the San Juan Island side of the channel when the rips are present.

Not intended for navigation

good and bad features of similar one-industry towns of that era.

In 1897 John S set up a subsidiary company to manufacture staveless barrels. A barrel factory was built on the point across from the east end of Pearl Island, where Neil Tarte's beautiful home now stands. Some 4,000 barrels a day were turned out; some were used for shipping the lime, while others were sold. The barrel factory burned down as the result of arson by a disgruntled employee. During the prohibition days of the 1920s, a Coast Guard station was located on the point.

The McMillins had four children. Each was given the middle name of Hiett, Mrs. McMillin's maiden name. The first, John, died at birth in 1878; Fred was born in 1880 and died in 1922; Paul was born in 1886 and died in 1961; and a daughter, Dorothy, was born in 1894.

John S built his own home on the waterfront, where the family could enjoy the magnificent view across the harbor. Today this building houses the resort's restaurant and lounge. Mrs. McMillin supervised the planting and care of the lovely flower garden adjacent to their island home.

Sunsets at Roche Harbor are something special. Long after the bronze sun has said a reluctant goodnight and sunk behind the hills and mountains of Vancouver Island, an afterglow continues to paint the western sky. Partly to take advantage of this spectacular display, a fine home was built for Fred McMillin near the beach around the point looking over Spieden Channel. The home was named Afterglow Manor. After Fred's death the home was used by the rest of the family. In 1944 a fire, caused by an electrical short circuit, burned the home to the ground.

Fred McMillin was his father's favorite and had been groomed to take over the business. His death was a great shock to John S, who grieved for many years afterward. Younger brother Paul, who had been a salesman for the company, took over as general manager but there was constant disagreement between Paul and his father.

DAVE CALHOUN

LEFT: You can't buy lime and cement there anymore, but the building does house a well-stocked general grocery.

BELOW: The Roche Harbor store occupies this building at the head of the dock.

DAVE CALHOUN

John S had a 50-foot yacht, the *Calcite*, which he moored at the small-craft float in front of his home. The yacht was used for short trips through the islands and longer vacation cruises, one of which is documented in Volume I of *Northwest Passages*. A story is told that the boys and some of their pals occasionally would take the yacht on an alleged trip to Victoria for a golf game. When John S discovered that they were anchoring in nearby Garrison Bay for a night or weekend of cards and drinking, he had a golf course built adjacent to the town so there would no longer be an excuse for such excursions.

Fire swept the entire waterfront in 1923, razing much of the lime plant, warehouse, dock, and store. McMillin promptly rebuilt the structures, modernizing them throughout and installing new equipment.

Although John S expended much energy and effort on his business and political affairs, he did not neglect the social side of life.

John S McMillin, who developed the lime company and much of the town that grew up around it.

He liked nothing better than to entertain his friends and business associates at huge feasts held in the banquet court next to the hotel, or to transport them by barge to McCracken Point on Henry Island for a noontime salmon barbecue. Any holiday or special occasion was an excuse for such an affair, and at one such barbecue on the point, some 1,100 guests were served in grand style.

On many a summer evening, two of the company barges, gaily decorated with fir trees and Chinese lanterns, were towed out into the bay. Guests danced on one barge to music from an orchestra playing on the other barge.

John McMillin ruled his dukedom, as some called it, with an iron hand, and he was accused of being a completely heartless, selfish dictator. But for every story of his tyranny, there is an account of some kindness or special concern and treatment accorded an employee.

McMillin had his own personal troubles, including a lawsuit charging him with fraud and mismanagement in his conduct of company affairs. During the two years that the case dragged on, both the local and the Seattle papers made many charges against him, including that of political bossism. In the end he was fully vindicated, but the adverse publicity had done much harm both to his political and his business life. He dropped out of public life and devoted more and more time to his business and to his family and home.

In the early 1930s, John S turned one of his dreams into partial reality. He designed and built a family mausoleum on the hill in back of Afterglow Manor. One of the family's pleasures was to sit around the dining room table after dinner and enjoy the sunset. He envisioned this practice continuing after death and incorporated the idea in the family memorial.

As a steadfast Mason, he used the symbolism of Masonry in his overall design to show his love and respect for the order as well as for

McMillin's banquet court (adjacent to the Hotel de Haro) as it looked in 1925.

God, country, and mankind. The structure consists of seven 30-foot Tuscan columns of the same diameter and circumference as those in King Solomon's temple. The columns are joined at the top by an encircling ring signifying eternal life after death. The ring was intended to support a bronze dome with a Maltese cross. A broken column on the west side represents the broken column of life and the unfinished state of man's work when the string of life is broken.

The winding stairs as a whole are representative of the mental and spiritual life: learning, studying, enlarging mental horizons, and increasing spiritual outlook. The stairs wind to symbolize the fact that man does not know what the future holds for him as he goes through life.

The stairs are in three tiers consisting of three, five, and seven steps. The three steps represent the three principal states of human life: youth, manhood, and age. In youth one should fill his mind with useful knowledge; in manhood one should apply that knowledge to the discharge of respective duties to God, neighbors, and oneself so that in age one may enjoy reflecting on a well-spent life and die in the hope of a glorious immortality.

The five steps represent the five orders in architecture: Tuscan, Doric, Ionic, Corinthian, and Composite, as well as the five human senses of hearing, seeing, feeling, smelling, and tasting.

The seven steps represent the seven liberal arts and sciences: grammar, rhetoric, logic, arithmetic, geometry, music, and astronomy. They also are the symbol that God created the earth in six days and rested on the seventh.

On a raised platform in the center of the columns is a round limestone and cement table surrounded by six chairs. The chairs, serving as crypts for the ashes of family members, are arranged as were those in the family dining room, where everyone seated at the table could see the view. Thus it was arranged that, in the symbolic

BELOW AND OPPOSITE: Guests at one of the barbecues hosted by McMillin in the banquet court and nearby grove.

reunion after death, the sun would shine on the family through the open spaces in the broken column.

John S completed the mausoleum in the spring of 1936. He died in November of the same year, so he was the first of the family to be laid to rest there. Mrs. McMillin died in 1943.

For financial reasons the bronze dome was never built to complete the structure. And in the years following the death of John S, the Northwest's lush growth of trees and shrubs all but engulfed the mausoleum. Some clearing now has been done, however, and more is planned. In recent years the Masons have taken an interest in the maintenance of this unique memorial.

As with most people, John S had his ups and downs. He dreamed and achieved even while beset with criticism, trials, and tribulations. He lived according to his ideals and the spirit of the times. His virtues and faults alike belonged to his era, an era that had its own problems and its own economic and social values, and he cannot be judged fairly outside the context of those times. However, he enjoyed a full

and successful life and certainly left an important heritage in the history of this portion of the San Juan Islands.

After his father's death, Paul McMillin continued to operate the lime company, although on a much reduced scale. Lacking the dynamic personality of his father, he became increasingly reclusive. I recall coming into the harbor about 1949. Paul met me at the wharf with a shotgun cradled in his arms and coldly announced that visitors were not welcome.

In 1956 the late Reuben J. Tarte of Seattle was more successful in effecting a friendly landing in his yacht *Clareu*. Paul took a liking

This photo shows the office of the Roche Harbor Lime and Cement Company, and the homes of McMillin and the plant superintendent.

to Tarte and subsequently sold him the company, the town, and 40,000 acres of land comprising the McMillin holdings.

With the same drive and energy that characterized John S, the Tarte family set about turning Roche Harbor into the lovely resort it is today. They rebuilt the inside of the Hotel de Haro and restored the outside so that it looks as it did when Teddy Roosevelt stayed there. They built a laundromat and showers, installed floats that will moor up to 250 boats, reopened the store and post office, converted the McMillin home into a fine restaurant, completely rebuilt and renovated the church, turned the old workers' homes and schoolhouse into housekeeping cottages, built a swimming pool, and generally cleaned up the entire place, to make it one of the finest resorts in the Northwest.

While Reuben and his sons and sons-in-law were hard at work, Clara Tarte was not idle. She restored and rebuilt the neglected flower garden and subsequently took many awards at local shows and fairs with her prize-winning blooms.

Mrs. Tarte also undertook the restoration of the church. Serving first as a Methodist church, then later as a schoolhouse, the structure was badly deteriorated when the Tartes took over. After the building was reconstructed, an altar was brought up from an old church in Kirkland, and pews were

The old office as it appears today, converted to a restaurant and cozy lounge.

DAVE CALHOUN

A view of Roche Harbor in its heyday as a lime-producing center.

Inside the Roche Harbor church , showing the altar.

The statue of Our Lady of Good Voyage, for whom the chapel is named.

The Chapel of Our Lady of Good Voyage, as it appears today.

purchased from a White Center church. The statue of Our Lady of Good Voyage, for whom the present family-owned Catholic chapel is named, was made in Italy at a cost of $600. Recently, carillon bells were dedicated to the memory of Reuben Tarte, who died in 1968, and son-in-law Robert Tangney, who was killed in a fireworks barge accident on July 4, 1971.

Clara Tarte also made a brief entry into the movie world. In 1966 Mrs. Tarte played a leading part in *Namu, the Killer Whale*, which was filmed in and around Roche Harbor.

The Tartes continued to operate the lime company, but only long enough to fulfill contracts and until the machinery broke down. Since then all their efforts have been toward building the resort. In 1989

DAVE CALHOUN

The family mausoleum, built by McMillin, stands on a hill near his home.

the Tartes sold the resort to local resident Verne Howard, who has many plans for future development. Behind the plans, however, is an underlying desire to maintain the richly flavored mood of the past. The restaurant has already been changed and modernized, but the visitor will hardly notice any changes in the overall appearance of the old McMillin residence.

Parts of the old warehouse and pier already have been torn down. A new store, showers, laundry facility, and gift shop are available for the yachtsman.

More than a century has passed since Joe Ruff filed his homestead claim at Roche Harbor. It was an interesting and often exciting 100 years that left many ghosts in the area. These ghosts still play a fascinating part in producing that inexplicable mood and distinctive aura that permeates today's Roche Harbor, adding even more to the magic of the islands.

When you finish reading the history of the area, stretch your legs along the shore. An inspection of the old kilns and diggings is always interesting. And it does not take much imagination to put the workers back in the pits, the steam engine and string of rock-loaded cars back on the tracks, the fires back in the kilns, and to see the whole place buzzing with activity again.

On the way to the mausoleum is an old cemetery that has been nearly overgrown in recent decades. But cleanup has been started and is to continue. A few years ago Rube Tarte told me a touching story about a lime plant worker's son who was drowned during a scuffle with an Indian boy. The son was buried in the cemetery in a grave marked by a little fawn. Later, the mother, then widowed, made yearly pilgramages from Seattle to place fresh flowers on her son's grave. It was impossible to learn if she still does this.

You can combine the hike to the mausoleum with a hike to Afterglow Manor by taking a trail that leads from the back of the mausoleum and exits in the vicinity of the site where Afterglow Manor once stood. While inspecting the ruins of the foundation, you may wonder about several large steel tanks. Paul McMillin told the Tartes that his mother did not like to wash her hair in the town's hard mineral water, so a massive system was installed to catch rainwater. The water was stored in these steel tanks for Mrs. McMillin's shampoos.

By approaching the town on the road along the shore, you will see the remains of the old company tug. A little farther along, near the swimming pool, is an ancient log cabin. This cabin was the first home of the Scurr brothers when they came to Roche Harbor, and possibly of Joe Ruff, too. Here, again, a bit of imagination can bring alive one of the oldest ties with the past on these grounds.

A traditional colors ceremony ends a long and busy day. Young people working at the resort form a color guard that marches smartly to a mast atop the roof of the old warehouse. It is a non-military ceremony, but accorded full respect. Business ceases, no fuel is sold, service in the dining room and lounge is suspended, and all attention is focused on the flags. To the bugle call "Retreat," the San Juan Yacht Club pennant is lowered. Next, "To the Colors" brings down the Washington State flag, followed by the Canadian flag to the tune of "O, Canada." The British flag is lowered to "God Save the Queen," and, finally, the United States flag is lowered to a bugle's plaintive "Taps" and a cannon salute. Flags are carefully folded and the color guard retires.

The flag ceremony is held exactly at sunset each evening. It is followed by a weather forecast and announcement of current weather conditions.

Guests may then settle back at the dinner tables or aboard their boats to enjoy the storied sunset afterglow as another day comes to a close at historic Roche Harbor, a favorite of many a San Juan visitor.

After such a day, you are relaxed and at peace with the world. Your memory log is filled with Roche Harbor scenes and with experiences you will not forget. You will probably find, as so many others have, that an overnight stop at Roche Harbor is not long enough, and, as you end one day there, you will already be planning your return.

16

A STOP AT ROSARIO

The Rosario Mansion as it appears today, with
dining room, spa, and swimming pool.

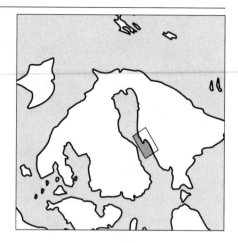

he story of the now-beautiful Rosario Resort on Orcas Island is really the story of a man named Robert Moran, and the tale has its beginnings on the Seattle waterfront more than 100 years ago.

Rain was falling on a cold November morning in 1875, when a ship from New York arrived at Yesler's Wharf in Seattle. After the regular passengers had disembarked, the steerage passengers came down the gangplank. Among them was Robert Moran, a 17-year-old, who clutched his bag of belongings as his eyes swept the nearly deserted waterfront. He was cold and hungry, and had only a dime in his pocket, which he knew would not buy much of a breakfast.

Robert Moran, third oldest of 10 children of an immigrant family, had joined the "Go West" movement to seek his fortune. He arrived in Seattle without friends, job, or place to live—and without money.

Robert was not a lad given to depression or worry. There was too much to be done. He set out up the muddy street until he was met suddenly by the unmistakable aroma of frying bacon and eggs, pancakes, and fresh coffee. A sign over the door read "Our House." Robert went into the pioneer eatery and talked proprietor Bill Grose, a huge, genial man, into a line of credit. Robert promptly downed a generous breakfast.

Grose tipped Robert off that a logging camp across the hill on Lake Washington was looking for a cook. Although Robert's talents lay in directions other than cooking, he needed a job. He made the long hike to the camp. But three days of Robert's cooking was all the loggers could stand, so the job ended abruptly and he began the lengthy trip back over the hill to Seattle.

During the next few years, Robert Moran had a succession of jobs, each a little better than the last. One such job was as a deckhand on the *J.B. Libby*, a sidewheeler that carried mail and supplies between Seattle and Bellingham by way of the San Juan Islands, and later destined to burn when her cargo of Roche Harbor lime caught fire. As the *Libby* steamed through the majestic passages between the islands and Robert got his first good look at them, he vowed, "Someday I'm going to live on one of these islands."

Robert was a thrifty lad. He saved his money until he had enough to bring his mother, brothers, and sisters to Seattle. He continued to improve his position and increase his savings until he had better than

The Rosario Mansion as it appeared during the time of Robert Moran.

$1,500. He then felt it was time to start out on his own, so with his savings he opened a marine repair business on the waterfront.

By 1889 Moran had built his business up to some $40,000 and had been elected mayor of Seattle, a post he held for two terms. While 1889 was a year of achievement for the erstwhile immigrant boy, it was also a year of disaster. In June a fire leveled much of Seattle, including Robert Moran's establishment. As mayor, it fell to him to make the unpleasant decision to dynamite several downtown blocks to keep the flames from taking the entire city.

Moran wasn't a man to be defeated. Like most of Seattle's businessmen, he started at once to rebuild. He enlarged his facilities,

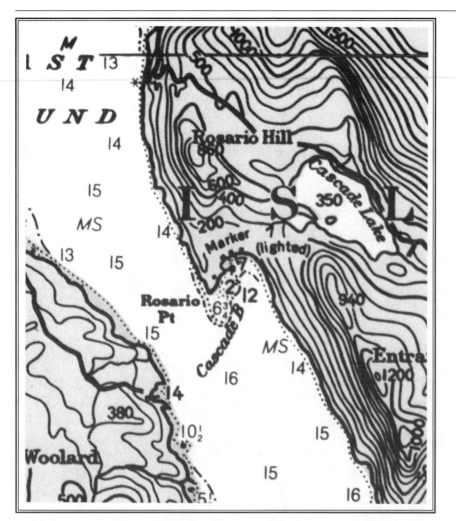

Rosario Point. The Rosario Resort overlooks Cascade Bay and East Sound. Dock space is available with reservations. If anchored, skippers should be sure the hook is well-set, and will remain set during a wind change.

Not intended for navigation

however, so that he could include shipbuilding. The crowning achievement of his yard was building the first-class battleship U.S.S. *Nebraska*, the largest vessel to be built on Puget Sound at that time. He was now one of the town's wealthiest and most influential citizens.

Ambition, drive, and hard work took their toll. By 1904 Moran had developed a serious heart condition. His doctors told him he would have to ease up at once and gave him six months to a year to live. Being a man of action, he immediately sold his shipyard. Then he could fulfill his boyhood vow, so he moved to Orcas Island. Moran purchased property on East Sound's Cascade Bay from Andrew Newhall, who operated the Cascade Lumber Company mill and box factory there.

With his penchant for hard work, Moran began to build his retirement home. He set up a hydroelectric plant and a machine shop and installed electric lights. He designed his own house, acted as contractor and foreman, and saw that it was built exactly as he wanted it.

This was no overnight job. Blasting the solid bedrock for a foundation, Moran made the first two stories of one-foot-thick concrete, with frame construction of the third floor. Six tons of copper sheets were used on the roof. Windows of 7/8-inch-thick porthole plate glass were set without frames into the walls. Moran used rare hardwood paneling and solid handmade African mahogany doors with non-squeaking hinges of lignum vitae. His own craftsmen made the trim and much of the hardware.

Imported teakwood was used generously for the interior finish. The parquet flooring of all three stories reportedly took two years to lay. The huge fireplace in the living room (now used as a dining room) was set with hand-rubbed marble left over from the building of the *Nebraska*, and with tile said to have come from the old Union Railway Depot in Seattle.

Rosario as it appears today, with dock space for a limited number of boats.

PHOTO COURTESY OF ROSARIO RESORT

Moran, a lover of good music, built a music room that extended from the second to the third floor. At a cost of $16,000, he installed a giant Aeolian organ with 1,972 pipes. The console was placed in a balcony of the room, along with a library. From Brussels Moran imported a lovely stained-glass window depicting the Antwerp harbor and protected it with specially designed shutters.

It has been said that frequently in the mornings Moran woke his guests with music from the mighty organ. The organ was equipped with a player piano device, and the story goes that sometimes, when guests relaxed to the strains of a Brahms or Beethoven classic in the music room, they could see Moran's head as he sat at the console, presumably fingering the keyboard. Actually, he was getting music from the player rolls. The pipe organ and Moran's Steinway grand piano are still there, and today Rosario offers an informative historical presentation featuring original Moran photographs and the playing of the Aeolian pipe organ and the grand piano in the music room.

On the lower floor Moran built a heated swimming pool, game rooms with billiard tables, a pair of bowling alleys, and a cabaret theater. Around the pool and in the game room the floors were laid with imported Italian mosaic tiles.

While the house was under construction the grounds were not neglected. Extensive gardens were planted with all manner of local and exotic flowers and shrubs. A 360-foot lagoon was dug and filled with trout, and a boat landing was built in the bay. Sidewalks and paved roadways were put in and lined with electric lights similar to those used in cities.

With a feeling for history, Moran built his own museum and filled it with artifacts he had collected. In 1915 he journeyed to Puerto Rico to bring back the salvaged figurehead from the wreck of the clipper ship *America*. This figurehead, carved in 1874 from a single pine log, was to become part of a yacht he planned to build. However, he decided it would be more appropriate as a lawn decoration looking out over the bay. It can be seen there today. When the battleship *Nebraska* was scrapped in 1923, Moran obtained one of her heavy anchor chains and used it to encircle the inner portion of the circular driveway at the entrance to the mansion.

At last the impressive 54-room mansion was completed, with a mix of 18 sleeping rooms, two-bedroom suites and bedroom-sitting room suites, each of them tastefully and luxuriously furnished. Naming his estate Rosario for the strait just across the island, Moran was proud of the showplace he had created. He appreciated the interest and curiosity of islanders and tourists, so he scheduled one day a week for open house and usually conducted the tour himself. The practice came to an end, however, when a tour party being shown Mrs. Moran's private bathroom came upon an unidentified young lady taking a bath there.

During the years of construction, Moran quietly purchased property around his original estate until he owned more than 7,000 acres, including Cascade Lake and Mt. Constitution. In 1921 he deeded some 6,000 acres of the land to the state for a recreational park known today as Moran State Park. His philanthropy, benefiting so many, included donations of several roads to the state or county, along with the machinery used to build them. Moran also shared his water rights with the community of Olga and assisted in building its water system.

The magic of the islands worked wonders for Moran. In spite of the doctor's gloomy prediction that in 1904 Moran had less than a year to live he continued to be active. He absorbed the healing peace and quiet of this paradise and lived almost 40 years longer to reach age 86.

After the death of his wife in the late 1930's, Moran sold the estate to Donald Rheems for a Depression figure of $50,000. In 1958 the Falcon Corporation of Waco, Texas, purchased it, built seven homes, put in a new water system, and subdivided part of the property.

In 1960 Seattle hardware merchant Gilbert Geiser, mayor of Mountlake Terrace, bought Rosario. A man of vision and imagination, Geiser, with his wife and the help of a loyal crew, set about converting the property into the magnificent resort it is today.

The undertaking was not an easy one. With the short boating and tourist summer season, the first few years were difficult. As Gil said one time, "There were periods when we weren't sure whether Rosario belonged to us or to the bank and creditors." Perseverance and hard work won out, however, and the result is one of the finest resorts in the country.

The Moran mansion is now the main lodge, where visitors can peek into one of Moran's guest rooms and can enjoy the gracious luxuries of the rich Oriental rugs, furnishings, music room, or indoor swimming pool, and satisfy their palates with excellent meals prepared by a top-notch chef. Also a spa has been integrated into the mansion's lower level.

Hughes Bay

In recent years cottage cabanas have been built to provide additional accommodations for visitors overlooking the boats coming and going on the bay.

The yachtsman is welcomed, directed to a moorage, and assisted in tying up by a dock boy. The popularity of Rosario and its dining facilities and limited moorage space make reservations a necessity. To avoid disappointment, make them at least two weeks in advance. I was unable to get in on two different occasions.

Today, moorage consists of the main dock with buoys out in the bay. Slips are limited, so advance reservations are required. Buoys are available on a first-come, first-served basis.

The dining room, several different-sized meeting rooms, and another outdoor swimming pool, this pool for adults only, were added to the main lodge. Rosario's meals are justly famous, but the Friday night seafood buffet is perhaps the most popular item on the menu. Meals are served in a beautifully appointed room that is tiered so that every guest has an unobstructed view of the pool and the expanse of East Sound. Live music is the latest addition, and has added much to

This elegant figurehead, brought to Rosario by Robert Moran, still sets the tone for the resort.

the resort's summertime appeal. Rosario is a favorite for small conventions, seminars, sales and business meetings in the off-season.

At the moorage basin are a snack shop, grocery store, showers, and laundromat. Ice is available, and fuel, oil, and water are found at the entrance to the basin. Another feature is the Discovery House, an 8,500-square-foot facility that serves as a convention center and as a nightclub for dinner and dancing. It has an open-pit barbecue and books top professional entertainment in the summer.

There are so many things to do at Rosario that it is almost impossible to list the activities. Adults can relax and visit, and the entire family can beachcomb for driftwood or agates, hike through the lovely countryside, play golf at a nearby course, fish in Cascade Lake, or rent a car to drive to the top of Mt. Constitution. There, from a lookout tower, they will find a truly spectacular panorama of all the islands. Mopeds can be rented, although they are not allowed on the road to Mt. Constitution.

While the summer season is its busiest, Rosario is really geared for year-round enjoyment. Since most Northwest yachtsmen do not decommission their boats for the winter, more and more skippers come to Rosario during the off-season for a "mood" weekend away, a holiday cruise, or a try for those winter blackmouth that locals claim are providing better winter fishing here than ever before. If winter cruising does not appeal, it is possible to go by combination of car and ferry, then charter a boat at the resort, and still enjoy a fishing trip. Special rates for all facilities are offered during the off-season.

No matter what your favorites may be in cruising the San Juans, a stop at Rosario should be a part of the visitor's itinerary.

17

A DAY IN THE SAN JUANS

Friday Harbor, looking northwest, with Brown Island on the right. Ample transient moorage is available, and the harbormaster often can direct visitors to the slips of permanent moorage residents who are away.

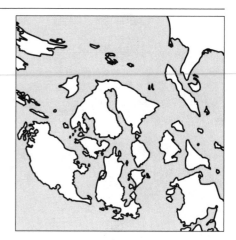

It is dawn in the San Juans. Faint light begins to seep over the distant mountains, expunging the dark of night from the eastern horizon. Imperceptibly, daylight increases. Striated oranges and reds take over the sky, setting the stage for the arrival of the sun.

Finally the sunrise washes away the shadows along the shore of our private cove, a quiet place where a blue sky scattered with powder-puff clouds is reflected in a mirror of glossy water.

The tang of salt air mixed with the aroma of bacon and coffee greets us as we prepare for another day of sampling the heady magic of the San Juans. The engine is started and the exhaust gargles in its throat as the anchor is taken up. Soon our bow wave is smiling, sending its long fingers out to investigate the shore, while the propeller lays out a foaming white path behind us.

Long, gently curving channels are our roadway leading to the everchanging passages between the islands. The San Juans are a fairyland of enchantment, a patchwork of north woods thrust up from an inland sea. We cruise through waters which are warm, rich, and two-toned, a light green over the shoals fading into a dark blue in the deep. Narrow passes are negotiated to the raucous cry of herons arguing about the right of way. There is a moment of excitement as the boat passes through the confused, giggling waters of a tide rip.

Although our charted course is a meandering line through passages and channels, the bow seems to turn magnetically into the many idyllic little coves and placid bays along the way that seem to whisper "explore me" in the skipper's ear. We slow the throttle, turn on the depth sounder, and add more entries to the logbook as we find spectacular hidden beauties: a cove with a quiet beach piled up with drift logs or an inland trail winding through the thick foliage of fir and cedar. The sunlight filters through the foliage in long shafts as from the stained-glass windows of a cathedral.

Another delight is leaving the main channel to swing in behind a small island to investigate what lies beyond. We are invariably rewarded with a discovery of still more scenic wonders reserved for those adventurous enough to stray off the usual courses.

Suddenly the morning is gone. The bright, shadowless world says it is past noon. The water is a light robin's egg blue spangled with gold as we drop anchor in the next bay. A grassy headland above a pebbled

A generation ago the boats looked different from those of today, but the charm of cruising in the San Juans remains unchanged. All rafted up in Echo Bay, these families are enjoying themselves.

beach issues an invitation to a shoreside picnic lunch. The sun is warm; the water, lightly dimpled, reflects an upside-down shoreline, while two gulls, their wing flaps down, are suspended in the sky. They wonder if we will share our lunch with them.

A crab trap is set. Cold cuts, cheese, crackers, and salad are laid out. Cold beer and pop bottles perspire waiting for the hands of a thirsty crew. It is a lazy, hot day, so lunch in such a wondrous setting is naturally followed by a brief, relaxing siesta. Lying on the green carpeting of the hillside, we listen to the wavelets polishing the smooth stones on the beach below. And to the harmonizing of the birds and the chattering of squirrels arguing over the ownership of a cache of nuts. Finally the inevitable urge for a nap takes over and we all doze peacefully.

It seems like only minutes before a whistle shatters the stillness to announce the arrival in the bay of friends who recognize our boat. After an exchange of where-have-you-been, what-have-you-been-doing, and where-are-you-heading, a decision is made to join forces for the rest of the day. The crab trap reveals a catch of four "keepers." With crab added to the other boat's ample collection of oysters and a freshly caught salmon, a fine seafood potluck dinner is promised.

We cruise for two more hours through the serenely beautiful waters of this vacation haven. We stop at Friday Harbor for some shopping, explore more coves, bays, and passages, and finally head for a harbor where state marine park buoys invite a safe and easy anchorage. Our friends raft their boat alongside.

Since clams are readily available here, we gather up shovels and pails, put on old sneakers dubbed "mudders," and set out in a pair of dinghies for the beach. An ebbing tide has sent much of the water in the bay to other shores, leaving great expanses of gray sand and gravel beach exposed. It does not take much excavating before we discover a well-populated community of tasty little bivalves. From an ever-lengthening trench we soon fill our buckets with littleneck and butter clams.

While the clams steam, surrendering that delicious nectar, the smaller oysters open their shells on the hibachi. A small slice of cheese placed on top of the meat and covered with a special barbecue sauce makes a delectable *hors d'oeuvre*. We must find a new way of preparing this tidbit because a recent state law requires that oysters be shucked at the place of taking and the shells left at the site. No gourmet chef could produce a more delicious meal from the food of the sea than we enjoy this night.

At 48.75 degrees north latitude plus an hour bonus from daylight saving time, the evenings are long in the San Juans. We sit languidly in the cockpit watching the activities in the harbor. A rising tide returns the water. The little waves, advancing ever higher, paint a scalloped border on the beach. The golden sun melts to bright orange as it hangs in the western sky, reluctant to leave for its long cruise across the Pacific. A mother duck maintains a protective position between us and her fleet of nervous babies as they seek the last scraps of food before they turn in for the night.

The setting sun spreads a watercolor montage of reds, oranges, and purples across the sky. A dinghy from another boat drifts by. They invite us to a campfire marshmallow roast ashore.

Joining a group already gathered around the beach fire, we find seats on a white drift log and are soon swapping cruising yarns with others of that friendly fraternity of yachtsmen. The protesting logs in the fire put on a miniature pyrotechnic display with pops and bangs, sending cascades of sparks into the darkness. The blue smoke hangs above us, perfuming the night air with a scent of pine. The younger crew members search out coals to roast their marshmallows and the inevitable guitar is produced for the songfest.

We are all silent as we row slowly back to the boats. The moon has come up full to siverplate everything in this charmed bay. The intoxication of night reminds us once again that there truly is magic in these San Juan Islands that cannot be denied.

Our boat rides peacefully at anchor. Our day in the San Juans ends. May your days there commence soon.

Two boats raft up in Shallow Bay, on the west side of Sucia Island.

San Juans
Place-Names
Index

This index of San Juans place-names is limited to localities within the San Juan archipelago and areas directly adjacent to and closely identified with the San Juans. Points enroute have not been indexed. This index is provided for the convenience of the reader who wishes to locate specific references or information quickly.

Cruise Notes:

Cruise Notes:

Turn Point Light

Cruise Notes:

Cruise Notes:

Ship's Figurehead, Rosario

Cruise Notes:

Pole Pass

Cruise Notes: